Great Military Commanders
Erwin Rommel
A Biography

Compiled by
Evelyn Stone

Scribbles

Year of Publication 2018

ISBN : 9789352979417

Book Published by

Scribbles

(An Imprint of Alpha Editions)

email - alphaedis@gmail.com

Produced by: PediaPress GmbH
Limburg an der Lahn
Germany
http://pediapress.com/

The content within this book was generated collaboratively by volunteers. Please be advised that nothing found here has necessarily been reviewed by people with the expertise required to provide you with complete, accurate or reliable information. Some information in this book may be misleading or simply wrong. Alpha Editions and PediaPress does not guarantee the validity of the information found here. If you need specific advice (for example, medical, legal, financial, or risk management) please seek a professional who is licensed or knowledgeable in that area.

Sources, licenses and contributors of the articles and images are listed in the section entitled "References". Parts of the books may be licensed under the GNU Free Documentation License. A copy of this license is included in the section entitled "GNU Free Documentation License"

The views and characters expressed in the book are those of the contributors and his/her imagination and do not represent the views of the Publisher.

Contents

Articles   **1**

Rommel   **1**
    Erwin Rommel 1

Rommel myth   **73**
    Rommel myth 73

Appendix   **107**
    References 107
    Article Sources and Contributors 128
    Image Sources, Licenses and Contributors 129

Article Licenses   **131**

Index   **133**

Rommel

Erwin Rommel

<indicator name="pp-autoreview"> </indicator>

Field Marshal
Erwin Rommel

(c. 1942)

Birth name	Johannes Erwin Eugen Rommel[1]
Nick-name(s)	"The Desert Fox"
Born	15 November 1891 Heidenheim, Württemberg, German Empire
Died	14 October 1944 (aged 52) Herrlingen, Württemberg, Nazi Germany
Buried	Cemetery of Herrlingen
Alle-giance	• German Empire (to 1918) • Weimar Republic (to 1933) • Nazi Germany (to 1944)
Service/-<wbr/->branch	• Army of Württemberg • *Reichsheer* • German Army

Years of service	1911–1944
Rank	*Generalfeldmarschall*
Commands held	• 7th Panzer Division • Afrika Korps • Panzer Army Africa • Army Group Africa • Army Group B

Battles/-wars	*See battles*
	World War I
	• First Battle of the Argonne (1915)
	• Masivul Lesului and Oituz Campaigns (1916–1917)
	• Battle of Caporetto (1917)
	
	World War II
	• Invasion of Poland
	• Fall of France
	  • Battle of Arras (1940)
	  • Siege of Lille (1940)
	• North African Campaign
	  • Operation Sonnenblume (1941)
	  • Siege of Tobruk (1941)
	  • Operation Brevity (1941)
	  • Operation Battleaxe (1941)
	  • Operation Crusader (1941)
	  • Battle of Gazala (1942)
	  • Battle of Bir Hakeim (1942)
	  • First Battle of El Alamein (1942)
	  • Battle of Alam Halfa (1942)
	  • Second Battle of El Alamein (1942)
	  • Battle of El Agheila (1942)
	  • Battle of the Kasserine Pass (1943)
	  • Battle of Medenine (1943)
	• Battle of Normandy (1944)

Awards	• Iron Cross, First Class • Pour le Mérite • Knight's Cross of the Iron Cross with Oak Leaves, Swords and Diamonds
Spouse(s)	Lucia Maria Mollin (m. 1916)
Relations	• Manfred Rommel (1928–2013), son • Gertrud Stemmer (1913–2000), daughter
Signature	

Erwin Rommel (15 November 1891 – 14 October 1944) was a German general and military theorist. Popularly known as the **Desert Fox**, he served as field marshal in the Wehrmacht of Nazi Germany during World War II.

Rommel was a highly decorated officer in World War I and was awarded the *Pour le Mérite* for his actions on the Italian Front. In 1937 he published his classic book on military tactics, *Infantry Attacks*, drawing on his experiences from World War I. In World War II, he distinguished himself as the commander of the 7th Panzer Division during the 1940 invasion of France. His leadership of German and Italian forces in the North African Campaign established his reputation as one of the most able tank commanders of the war, and earned him the nickname *der Wüstenfuchs*, "the Desert Fox". Among his British adversaries he earned a strong reputation for chivalry, and the North African campaign has often been called a "war without hate". He later commanded the German forces opposing the Allied cross-channel invasion of Normandy in June 1944.

Rommel supported the Nazi seizure of power and Adolf Hitler, although his reluctant stance towards antisemitism, Nazi ideology and level of knowledge of The Holocaust remain a matter of debate among scholars.[2,3,4,5,6] In 1944, Rommel was implicated in the 20 July plot to assassinate Hitler. Due to Rommel's status as a national hero, Hitler desired to eliminate him quietly instead of immediately executing him, as many other plotters were. Rommel was given a choice between committing suicide, in return for assurances that his reputation would remain intact and that his family would not be persecuted following his death, or facing a trial that would result in his disgrace and execution; he chose the former and committed suicide using a cyanide pill. Rommel was given a state funeral, and it was announced that he had succumbed to his injuries from the strafing of his staff car in Normandy.

Rommel has become a larger-than-life figure in both Allied and Nazi propaganda, and in postwar popular culture, with numerous authors considering him an apolitical, brilliant commander and a victim of the Third Reich although this assessment is contested by other authors as the Rommel myth. Rommel's reputation for conducting a clean war was used in the interest of the West German rearmament and reconciliation between the former enemies – the United Kingdom and the United States on one side and the new Federal Republic of Germany on the other. Several of Rommel's former subordinates, notably his chief of staff Hans Speidel, played key roles in German rearmament and integration into NATO in the postwar era. The German Army's largest military base, the Field Marshal Rommel Barracks, Augustdorf, is named in his honour.

Early life and career

Rommel was born on 15 November 1891 in Southern Germany at Heidenheim, 45 kilometres (28 mi) from Ulm, in the Kingdom of Württemberg, then part of the German Empire. He was the third of five children of Erwin Rommel Senior (1860–1913), a teacher and school administrator, and his wife Helene von Lutz, whose father Karl von Luz headed the local government council. As

Figure 1: *Lieutenant Rommel in Italy, 1917.*

a young man Rommel's father had been a lieutenant in the artillery. Rommel had one older sister, an art teacher who was his favorite sibling, one older brother named Manfred who died in infancy and two younger brothers, of whom one became a successful dentist and the other an opera singer.[7,8,9,10]

At age 18 Rommel joined the local 124th Württemberg Infantry Regiment as a *Fähnrich* (ensign), in 1910, studying at the Officer Cadet School in Danzig.[11] He graduated in November 1911 and was commissioned as a lieutenant in January 1912 and was assigned to the 124th Infantry in Weingarten.[12] He was posted to Ulm in March 1914 to the 46th Field Artillery Regiment, XIII (Royal Württemberg) Corps, as a battery commander. He returned to the 124th when war was declared.[13] While at Cadet School, Rommel met his future wife, 17-year-old Lucia (Lucie) Maria Mollin (1894–1971), of Polish and Italian descent.[14]

World War I

During World War I, Rommel fought in France as well as in the Romanian and Italian Campaigns. He successfully employed the tactics of penetrating enemy lines with heavy covering fire coupled with rapid advances, as well as moving forward rapidly to a flanking position to arrive at the rear of hostile positions, to achieve tactical surprise.[15] His first combat experience was on 22

August 1914 as a platoon commander near Verdun, when – catching a French garrison unprepared – Rommel and three men opened fire on them without ordering the rest of his platoon forward.[16] The armies continued to skirmish in open engagements throughout September, as the static trench warfare typical of the First World War was still in the future.[17] For his actions in September 1914 and January 1915, Rommel was awarded the Iron Cross, Second Class.[18] Rommel was promoted to *Oberleutnant* (first lieutenant) and transferred to the newly created Royal Wurttemberg Mountain Battalion of the *Alpenkorps* in September 1915, as a company commander.[19] In November 1916 in Danzig, Rommel and Lucia married.[20]

In August 1917, his unit was involved in the battle for Mount Cosna, a heavily fortified objective on the border between Hungary and Romania, which they took after two weeks of difficult uphill fighting.[21] The Mountain Battalion was next assigned to the Isonzo front, in a mountainous area in Italy. The offensive, known as the Battle of Caporetto, began on 24 October 1917.[22] Rommel's battalion, consisting of three rifle companies and a machine gun unit, was part of an attempt to take enemy positions on three mountains: Kolovrat, Matajur, and Stol.[23] In two and a half days, from 25 to 27 October, Rommel and his 150 men captured 81 guns and 9,000 men (including 150 officers), at the loss of six dead and 30 wounded.[24] Rommel achieved this remarkable success by taking advantage of the terrain to outflank the Italian forces, attacking from unexpected directions or behind enemy lines, and taking the initiative to attack when he had orders to the contrary. In one instance, the Italian forces, taken by surprise and believing that their lines had collapsed, surrendered after a brief firefight.[25] In this battle, Rommel helped pioneer infiltration tactics, a new form of maneuver warfare just being adopted by German armies, and later by foreign armies,[26,27] and described by some as Blitzkrieg without tanks.[28,29] He played no role in the early adoption of Blitzkrieg in World War II though.[29] Acting as advance guard in the capture of Longarone on 9 November, Rommel again decided to attack with a much smaller force. Convinced that they were surrounded by an entire German division, the 1st Italian Infantry Division – 10,000 men – surrendered to Rommel. For this and his actions at Matajur, he received the order of Pour le Mérite.[26]

In January 1918, Rommel was promoted to *Hauptmann* (captain) and assigned to a staff position with XLIV Army Corps, where he served for the remainder of the war.[30]

Between the wars

Rommel remained with the 124th Regiment until 1 October 1920, when he was named a company commander in the 13th Infantry Regiment in Stuttgart, a post he held with the rank of captain for the next nine years.[31,24] His regiment was involved in quelling riots and civil disturbances that were occurring throughout Germany at this time.[32] Wherever possible, he avoided the use of force in these confrontations.[33] He decided against storming the city of Lindau, which had been taken by revolutionary communists. Instead, Rommel negotiated with the city council and managed to return it to the legitimate government through diplomatic means.[3,34] This was followed by another bloodless defence of Schwäbisch Gmünd.[35] Historian Raffael Scheck praises Rommel for being a coolheaded and moderate mind, exceptional among the massive violence caused by takeovers of many revolutionary cities by regular and irregular units.[3] After that, he was posted to the Ruhr where a red army was responsible for fomenting unrest. This episode left an indelible impression on Rommel's mind, and also that of Hitler (like Rommel, he had also experienced the solidarity of trench warfare) who participated in the suppression of the First and Second Bavarian Soviet Republics by the Reichswehr, that, according to Reuth, "Everyone in this Republic was fighting each other", and that there were people trying to convert Germany into a socialist republic on the Soviet lines. The need for national unity thus became a decisive legacy of the first World War.[34]

He was assigned as an instructor at the Dresden Infantry School from 1929 to 1933, and was promoted to major in April 1932.[24,36] While at Dresden, he wrote a manual on infantry training, published in 1934. Rommel was promoted to *Oberstleutnant* (lieutenant colonel) in October 1933, and given his next command, the 3rd *Jäger* Battalion, 17th Infantry Regiment, stationed at Goslar.[37] Here he first met Hitler, who inspected his troops on 30 September 1934.[38] In September 1935 Rommel was moved to the War Academy at Potsdam as an instructor, a post he held for the next three years.[39] His book *Infanterie greift an* (*Infantry Attacks*), a description of his wartime experiences along with his analysis, was published in 1937. It became a bestseller, which, according to Scheck, later "enormously influenced" many armies of the world;[3,40] Adolf Hitler was one of many people who owned a copy.[41]

Hearing of Rommel's reputation as an outstanding military instructor, in February 1937 Hitler assigned him as the War Ministry liaison officer to the Hitler Youth, in charge of military training. Here he clashed with Baldur von Schirach, the Hitler Youth leader, over the training that the boys should receive.[42,43,44,45,46] Trying to fulfill a mission assigned to him by the Ministry of War,[47] Rommel had proposed a plan (twice) that would have effectively subordinated Hitler Youth to the army, removing it from the NSDAP control.

Figure 2: *Rommel and Adolf Hitler in Goslar, 1934*

That went against Schirach's express wishes, who appealed directly to Hitler. Consequently, Rommel was quietly removed from the project in 1938.[48] He was promoted to *Oberst* (colonel) on 1 August 1937, and in 1938, Rommel was appointed commandant of the Theresian Military Academy at Wiener Neustadt.[49] In October 1938 Hitler specially requested that Rommel be seconded to command the *Führerbegleitbatallion* (his escort battalion).[50] This unit accompanied him whenever he traveled outside of Germany.[38] During this period he indulged his interest in engineering and mechanics by learning about the inner workings and maintenance of internal combustion engines and heavy machine guns.[51] He memorized logarithm tables in his spare time, and enjoyed skiing and other outdoor sports.[52]

World War II

Poland 1939

Rommel was promoted to *Generalmajor* on 23 August 1939 and assigned as commander of the *Führerbegleitbatallion*, tasked with guarding Hitler and his field headquarters during the invasion of Poland, which began on 1 September.[53] Hitler took a personal interest in the campaign, often moving close to the front in the *Führersonderzug* (headquarters train).[54] Rommel attended Hitler's

Figure 3: *Hitler in Poland (September 1939). Rommel is on his left and Martin Bormann on his right.*

daily war briefings and accompanied him everywhere, making use of the opportunity to observe first-hand the use of tanks and other motorized units.[55] On 26 September Rommel returned to Berlin to set up a new headquarters for his unit in the Reich Chancellery.[56] Rommel returned briefly to Warsaw on 5 October to organise the German victory parade. He described the devastated Warsaw in a letter to his wife, concluding with: "There has been no water, no power, no gas, no food for two days. They have erected numerous barricades which blocked civilian movement and exposed people to bombardments from which they could not escape. The mayor estimated the number of the dead and injured to be 40,000 ... The inhabitants probably drew a breath of relief that we have arrived and rescued them".[57,58]

France 1940

Panzer Division commander

Following the campaign in Poland, Rommel began lobbying for command of one of Germany's panzer divisions, of which there were then only ten.[59] Rommel's successes in World War I were based on surprise and maneuver, two elements for which the new panzer units were ideally suited.[60] Rommel received a promotion to a general's rank from Hitler ahead of more senior officers. Rommel obtained the command he aspired to, despite having been earlier turned down by the army's personnel office, which had offered him command of a

Figure 4: *General Erwin Rommel and his staff observe troops of the 7th Panzer Division practicing a river crossing at the Moselle River in France in 1940.*

mountain division instead.[61] According to Caddick-Adams, he was backed by Hitler, the influential Fourteenth Army commander Wilhelm List (a fellow Württemberger middle-class "military outsider") and likely Guderian as well.[62]

Going against military protocol, this promotion added to Rommel's growing reputation as one of Hitler's favoured commanders,[63] although his later outstanding leadership in France quelled complaints about his self-promotion and political scheming.[64] The 7th Panzer Division had recently been converted to an armoured division consisting of 218 tanks in three battalions (thus, one tank regiment, instead of the two assigned to a standard panzer division),[65] with two rifle regiments, a motorcycle battalion, an engineer battalion, and an anti-tank battalion.[66] Upon taking command on 10 February 1940, Rommel quickly set his unit to practicing the maneuvers they would need in the upcoming campaign.[67]

Invasion of the Netherlands, Belgium and France

The invasion began on 10 May 1940 with the bombardment of Rotterdam. By the third day Rommel and the advance elements of his division, together with a detachment of the 5th Panzer Division under Colonel Hermann Werner, had reached the River Meuse, where they found the bridges had already been destroyed (Guderian and Reinhardt reached the river on the same day).[68] Rommel was active in the forward areas, directing the efforts to make a crossing, which were initially unsuccessful due to suppressive fire by the French on the other side of the river. Rommel brought up tanks and flak units to provide counter-fire and had nearby houses set on fire to create a smokescreen. He sent infantry across in rubber boats, appropriated the bridging tackle of the 5th Panzer Division, personally grabbed a light machine gun to fight off a French counterattack supported by tanks, and went into the water himself, encouraging the sappers and helping lash together the pontoons.[69,70] By 16 May Rommel reached Avesnes, and contravening all orders and doctrine, he pressed on to Cateau.[71] That night, the French II Army Corps was shattered and on 17 May, Rommel's forces took 10,000 prisoners, losing 36 men in the process. He was surprised to find out only his vanguard had followed his tempestuous surge. The High Command and Hitler had been extremely nervous about his disappearance, although they awarded him the Knight's Cross. Rommel's (and Guderian's) successes and the new possibilities offered by the new tank arm were welcomed by a small number of generals, but worried and paralysed the rest.[72]

Battle of Arras

On 20 May Rommel reached Arras.[73] General Hermann Hoth received orders that the town should be bypassed and its British garrison thus isolated. He ordered the 5th Panzer Division to move to the west and 7th Panzer Division to the east, flanked by the SS Division *Totenkopf*.[74] The following day the British launched a counterattack, meeting the SS *Totenkopf* with two infantry battalions supported by heavily armoured Matilda Mk I and Matilda II tanks in the Battle of Arras. The German 37 mm anti-tank gun proved ineffective against the heavily armoured Matildas. The 25th Panzer Regiment and a battery of 88 mm (3.5 in) anti-aircraft guns were called in to support, and the British withdrew.[75]

On 24 May, Field Marshal von Rundstedt and Field Marshal von Kluge issued a halt order, which Hitler approved. The reason for this decision is still a matter of debate.[76,77,78] The halt order was lifted on 26 May.[77] 7th Panzer continued its advance, reaching Lille on 27 May. For the assault, Hoth placed the 5th Panzer Division's Panzer Brigade under Rommel's command.[79] The Siege of Lille continued until 31 May, when the French garrison of 40,000

Figure 5: *Rommel and staff during the Battle for France, June 1940*

men surrendered. 7th Panzer was given six days leave, during which Rommel was summoned to Berlin to meet with Hitler. He was the only divisional commander present at the planning session for *Fall Rot* (Case Red), the second phase of the invasion of France. By this time the evacuation of the BEF was complete; over 338,000 Allied troops had been evacuated across the Channel, though they had to leave behind all their heavy equipment and vehicles.[80]

Drive for the Channel

Rommel, resuming his advance on 5 June, drove for the River Seine to secure the bridges near Rouen. Advancing 100 kilometres (62 mi) in two days, the division reached Rouen to find the bridges destroyed. On 10 June, Rommel reached the coast near Dieppe, sending Hoth the laconic message "Bin an der Küste" or "Am on the coast".[81] On 17 June, 7th Panzer was ordered to advance on Cherbourg, where additional British evacuations were underway. The division advanced 240 kilometres (150 mi) in 24 hours, and after two days of shelling, the French garrison surrendered on 19 June.[82] The speed and surprise it was consistently able to achieve, to the point where both the enemy and the *Oberkommando des Heeres* (OKH; German High Command) at times lost track of its whereabouts, earned the 7th Panzers the nickname *Gespensterdivision* (Ghost Division).[83]

After the armistice with the French was signed on 22 June, the division was placed in reserve, being sent first to the Somme and then to Bordeaux to re-equip and prepare for *Unternehmen Seelöwe* (Operation Sea Lion), the planned invasion of Britain.[84] This invasion was later cancelled as Germany was not able to acquire the air superiority needed for a successful outcome, while the Kriegsmarine was massively outnumbered by the Royal Navy.[85]

Execution of prisoners in France

In France, Rommel ordered the execution of one French officer who refused three times to cooperate when being taken prisoner; there are disputes as to whether this execution was justified.[86] Bewley remarks that the shooting of a prisoner who does not behave as a prisoner is a legal option; however, this act was brutal because the officer did not have a gun, while Richard Weston, veteran at Tobruk, argues that it was not only legal but also made sense considering Rommel's situation. Caddick-Adams comments that this would make Rommel a war criminal condemned by his own hand, and that other authors overlook this episode.[87] French historian Petitfrère remarks that Rommel was in a hurry and had no time for useless palavers, although this act was still debatable. Telp remarks that, "For all his craftiness, Rommel was chivalrous by nature and not prone to order or condone acts of needless violence ... He treated prisoners of war with consideration. On one occasion, he was forced to order the shooting of a French lieutenant-colonel for refusing to obey his captors."[88] Scheck says, "Although there is no evidence incriminating Rommel himself, his unit did fight in areas where German massacres of black French prisoners of war were extremely common in June 1940."[89,90]

According to some authors, during the fighting in France, Rommel's 7th Panzer Division, alongside troops from 5th Panzer Division, committed numerous atrocities against French troops including the murder of 50 surrendering officers and men at Quesnoy and the nearby Airaines[91]</ref>[92]</ref>[93] After the war a memorial was erected to the commanding French officer Charles N'Tchoréré allegedly executed by soldiers under Rommel's command. The division is considered by Scheck to have been "likely" responsible for the execution of POW's in Hangest-sur-Somme,[94]</ref> while Scheck believes they were too far away to have been involved in the massacres at Airaines and nearby villages. French historian Dominique Lormier states the number of victims of 7th Panzer Division in Airaines at 109 mostly French-African soldiers from Senegal.[95] Historian Daniel Butler agrees that it was possible the massacre at Le Quesnoy happened given the existence of Nazis like Hanke in Rommel's division, while stating that in comparison with other German units, few sources regarding such actions of the men of the 7th Panzer exist (Butler believes that "it's almost impossible to imagine" Rommel authorizing or countenancing such actions, in either case[96]). Showalter claims there was no massacre at Le Quesnoy.[97] Claus Telp comments that Airaines was not in the sector of the 7th, but at Hangest and Martainville elements of the

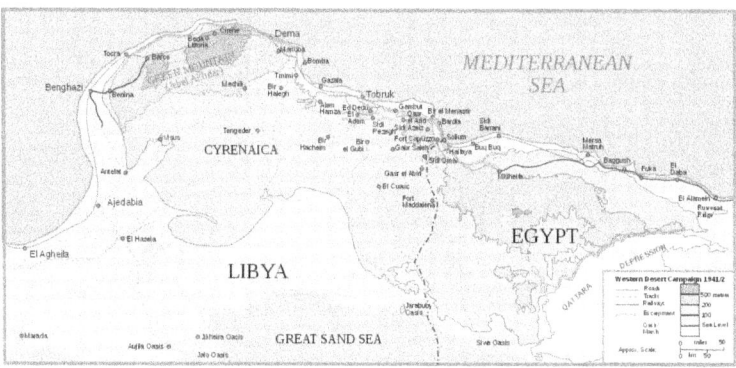

Figure 6: *Western Desert battle area*

7th might have shot some prisoners and used British Colonel Broomhall as a human shield (although Telp is of the opinion that it was unlikely Rommel approved or even knew about these two incidents).[98]

North Africa 1941–1943

On 6 February 1941, Rommel was appointed commander of the newly created *Deutsches Afrika Korps* (DAK), consisting of the 5th Light Division (later re-designated 21st Panzer Division) and of the 15th Panzer Division.[99] He was promoted to the rank of *Generalleutnant* three days later and flew to Tripoli on 12 February.[100] The DAK had been sent to Libya in Operation Sonnenblume, to support Italian troops that had been severely defeated by British Commonwealth forces in Operation Compass.[100] His efforts in the Western Desert Campaign earned Rommel the nickname the "Desert Fox" from British journalists.[101] Allied troops in Africa were commanded by General Archibald Wavell, Commander-in-Chief Middle East Command.[102]

First Axis offensive

Rommel and his troops were technically subordinate to Italian commander-in-chief General Italo Gariboldi.[99] Disagreeing with the Oberkommando der Wehrmacht (OKW)'s orders to assume a defensive posture along the front line at Sirte, Rommel resorted to subterfuge and insubordination to take the war to the British.[103] According to Remy, the General Staff tried to slow him down, but Hitler encouraged him to advance—an expression of the conflict which had existed between Hitler and the army leadership since the invasion of Poland.[104] He decided to launch a limited offensive on 24 March with 5th Light Division, supported by two Italian divisions.[105] This thrust was not anticipated by the

Figure 7: *Sd.Kfz. 6/1 with 88mm gun in tow, April 1941*

British, who had Ultra intelligence showing that Rommel had orders to remain on the defense until at least May, when the 15th Panzers were due to arrive.[106]

The British Western Desert Force had meanwhile been weakened by the transfer in mid-February of three divisions to help defend Greece.[107] They fell back to Mersa El Brega and started constructing defensive works.[108] Rommel continued his attack against these positions to prevent the British from building up their fortifications. After a day of fierce fighting on 31 March, the Germans captured Mersa El Brega.[109] Splitting his force into three groups, Rommel resumed the advance on 3 April. Benghazi fell that night as the British pulled out of the city.[110,111] Gariboldi, who had ordered Rommel to stay in Mersa El Brega, was furious. Rommel was equally forceful in his response, telling Gariboldi: "One cannot permit unique opportunities to slip by for the sake of trifles."[112] At that point a signal arrived from General Franz Halder reminding Rommel that he was to halt in Mersa El Brega. Knowing Gariboldi could not speak German, Rommel told him the message gave him complete freedom of action. Gariboldi backed down.[113]

On 4 April Rommel was advised by his supply officers that fuel was running short, which could result in a delay of up to four days. The problem was ultimately Rommel's fault, as he had not advised his supply officers of his intentions, and no fuel dumps had been set up. Rommel ordered the 5th Light Division to unload all their lorries and return to El Agheila to collect fuel and ammunition. Driving through the night, they were able to reduce the halt to a single day. Fuel supply was problematic throughout the campaign, as no petrol was available locally; it had to be brought from Europe via tanker and then carried by road to where it was needed.[114,115] Food and fresh water were also in short supply, and it was difficult to move tanks and other equipment

Figure 8: *Afrika Korps Panzer III advances past a vehicle burning in the desert, April 1941*

off-road through the sand.[116] In spite of these problems, Cyrenaica was captured by 8 April, except for the port city of Tobruk, which was surrounded on the landward sides on 11 April.[117,118]

Siege of Tobruk

The siege of Tobruk was not technically a siege, as the defenders were still able to move supplies and reinforcements into the city via the port.[119] Rommel knew that by capturing the port he could greatly reduce the length of his supply lines and increase his overall port capacity, which was insufficient even for day-to-day operations and only half that needed for offensive operations.[120] The city, which had been heavily fortified by the Italians during their 30-year occupation, was garrisoned by the 18th Infantry Brigade of the Australian 7th Division, the Australian 9th Division, HQ 3rd Armoured Brigade, several thousand British infantrymen, and one regiment of Indian infantry, for a total of 36,000 men.[121] The commanding officer was Australian Lieutenant General Leslie Morshead.[122] Hoping to catch the defenders off-guard, Rommel launched a failed attack on 14 April.[123]

Rommel requested reinforcements, but the OKW, then completing preparations for Operation Barbarossa, refused.[124] General Friedrich Paulus, head of the Operations Branch of OKH, arrived on 25 April to review the situation.[125] He was present for a second failed attack on the city on 30 April. On 4 May Paulus ordered that no further attempts should be made to take Tobruk via a direct assault. This order was not open to interpretation, and Rommel had no choice but to comply.[126] Aware of this order from intelligence reports,

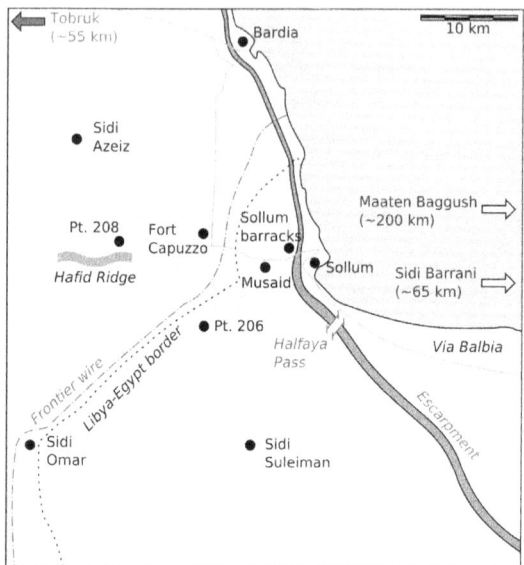

Figure 9: *Map of Halfaya Pass and surrounding area*

Churchill urged Wavell to seize the initiative. While awaiting further reinforcements and a shipment of 300 tanks that were already on their way, Wavell launched a limited offensive code named Operation Brevity on 15 May. The British briefly seized Sollum, Fort Capuzzo, and the important Halfaya Pass, a bottleneck along the coast near the border between Libya and Egypt. Rommel soon forced them to withdraw.[127,128] On 15 June Wavell launched Operation Battleaxe. The attack was defeated in a four-day battle at Sollum and Halfaya Pass, resulting in the loss of 98 British tanks. The Germans lost 12 tanks, while capturing and seriously damaging over 20 British tanks.[129] The defeat resulted in Churchill replacing Wavell with General Claude Auchinleck as theatre commander.[130] Rommel appointed Heinrich Kirchheim as commander of 5th Light Division on 16 May, became displeased and replaced him with Johann von Ravenstein on 30 May 1941.[131,132]

In August, Rommel was appointed commander of the newly created Panzer Group Africa, with Fritz Bayerlein as his chief of staff.[133] The Afrika Korps, comprising the 15th Panzer Division and the 5th Light Division, now reinforced and redesignated 21st Panzer Division, was put under command of Generalleutnant Ludwig Crüwell. In addition to the Afrika Korps, Rommel's Panzer Group had the 90th Light Division and four Italian divisions, three infantry divisions investing Tobruk, and one holding Bardia. The two Italian armoured divisions, *Ariete* and *Trieste*, were still under Italian control.

Figure 10: *8.8 cm (3 in) Flak 18 guns fire upon British armour*

They formed the Italian XX Motorized Corps under the command of General Gastone Gambara.[134] Two months later Hitler decided he must have German officers in better control of the Mediterranean theatre, and appointed Field Marshal Albert Kesselring as Commander in Chief, South. Kesselring was ordered to get control of the air and sea between Africa and Italy.[134]

Operation Crusader

Following his success in Battleaxe, Rommel returned his attention to the capture of Tobruk. He made preparations for a new offensive, to be launched between 15 and 20 November.[135] Meanwhile, Auchinleck reorganised Allied forces and strengthened them to two corps, XXX and XIII, which formed the British Eighth Army, which was placed under the command of Alan Cunningham. Auchinleck had 770 tanks and double the number of Axis aircraft.[136] Rommel opposed him with the 15th and 21st Panzer Divisions with a total of 260 tanks, the 90th Light Infantry division, five Italian infantry divisions, and one Italian armoured division of 278 tanks.[137,138]

Auchinleck launched Operation Crusader, a major offensive to relieve Tobruk, on 18 November 1941. The XIII Corps on the right were assigned to attack Sidi Omar, Capuzzo, Sollum, and Bardia; the XXX Corps (which included most of the armour) were to move on the left southern flank to a position about 30 miles (48 km) south of Tobruk, with the expectation that Rommel would find this move so threatening that he would move his armour there in response. Once Rommel's tanks were written down, the British 70th Infantry Division would

Figure 11: *Rommel conversing with his staff near El Agheila, 12 January 1942*

break out of Tobruk to link up with XXX Corps.[139,140] Rommel reluctantly decided on 20 November to call off his planned attack on Tobruk.[141]

Some elements of the 7th Armoured Division were stopped on the 19th by the Italian *Ariete* Armoured Division at Bir el Gobi, but they also managed to capture the airfields at Sidi Rezegh, 10 miles (16 km) from Tobruk.[142] Engaging the Allied tanks located there became Rommel's primary objective. Noting that the British armour was separated into three groups incapable of mutual support, he concentrated his Panzers so as to gain local superiority.[143] The expected breakout from Tobruk, which took place on 20 November, was stopped by the Italians. The airfield at Sidi Rezegh was retaken by 21st Panzer on 22 November. In four days of fighting, the Eighth Army lost 530 tanks and Rommel only 100.[144] The German forces near Halfaya Pass were cut off on 23 November.[144]

Wanting to exploit the British halt and their apparent disorganisation, on 24 November Rommel counterattacked near the Egyptian border in an operation that became known as the "dash to the wire". Unknown to Rommel, his troops passed within 6 kilometres (4 mi) of a major British supply dump. Cunningham asked Auchinleck for permission to withdraw into Egypt, but Auchinleck refused, and soon replaced Cunningham as commander of Eighth Army with Major General Neil Ritchie.[145,146] The German counterattack stalled as it outran its supplies and met stiffening resistance, and was criticised by the German High Command and some of Rommel's staff officers.[147]

Figure 12: *North Africa, Rommel in a Sd.Kfz. 250/3*

While Rommel drove into Egypt, the remaining Commonwealth forces east of Tobruk threatened the weak Axis lines there. Unable to reach Rommel for several days,[148]</ref> Rommel's Chief of Staff, Siegfried Westphal, ordered the 21st Panzer Division withdrawn to support the siege of Tobruk. On 27 November the British attack on Tobruk linked up with the defenders, and Rommel, having suffered losses that could not easily be replaced, had to concentrate on regrouping the divisions that had attacked into Egypt. By 7 December Rommel fell back to a defensive line at Gazala, just west of Tobruk, all the while under heavy attack from the Desert Air Force. The Bardia garrison surrendered on 2 January and Halfaya on 17 January 1942.[149] The Allies kept up the pressure, and Rommel was forced to retreat all the way back to the starting positions he had held in March, reaching El Agheila in December 1941.[150] The British had retaken almost all of Cyrenaica, but Rommel's retreat dramatically shortened his supply lines.[151]

Battle of Gazala and capture of Tobruk

Spring, 1942

On 5 January 1942 the Afrika Korps received 55 tanks and new supplies and Rommel started planning a counterattack. On 21 January, Rommel launched the attack.[152,153] Caught by surprise by the Afrika Korps, the Allies lost over 110 tanks and other heavy equipment. The Axis forces retook Benghazi on 29 January and Timimi on 3 February, with the Allies pulling back to a defensive line just before the Tobruk area south of the coastal town of Gazala.

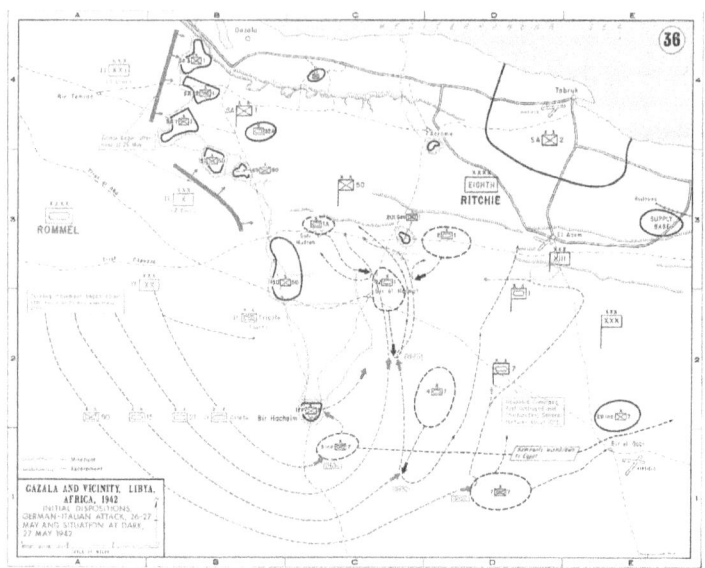

Figure 13: *Situation in "the Cauldron", 27 May 1942*

Rommel placed a thin screen of mobile forces before them, and held the main force of the Panzerarmee well back near Antela and Mersa Brega.[154] Between December 1941 and June 1942, Rommel had excellent information about the disposition and intentions of the Commonwealth forces. Bonner Fellers, the US diplomat in Egypt, was sending detailed reports to the US State Department using a compromised code.[155]

Following Kesselring's successes in creating local air superiority around the British naval and air bases at Malta in April 1942, an increased flow of supplies reached the Axis forces in Africa.[156] With his forces strengthened, Rommel contemplated a major offensive operation for the end of May. He knew the British were planning offensive operations as well, and he hoped to pre-empt them. While out on reconnaissance on 6 April, he was severely bruised in the abdomen when his vehicle was the target of artillery fire.[157] The British had 900 tanks in the area, 200 of which were new Grant tanks. Unlike the British, the Axis forces had no armoured reserve; all operable equipment was put into immediate service. Rommel's Panzer Army Africa had a force of 320 German tanks; 50 of these were the light Panzer II model. In addition, 240 Italian tanks were in service, but these were also under-gunned and poorly armoured.[158]

Early in the afternoon of 26 May 1942, Rommel attacked first and the Battle of Gazala commenced. Italian infantry supplemented with small numbers of armoured forces assaulted the centre of the Gazala fortifications. To give the impression that this was the main assault, spare aircraft engines mounted on trucks were used to create huge clouds of dust. Ritchie was not convinced by this display, and left the 4th and 22nd Armoured Brigades in position at the south end of the Commonwealth position.[159] Under the cover of darkness, the bulk of Rommel's motorized and armoured forces (15th and 21st Panzers, 90th Light Division, and the Italian Ariete and Trieste Divisions) drove south to skirt the left flank of the British, coming up behind them and attacking to the north the following morning.[160] Throughout the day a running armour battle occurred, where both sides took heavy losses. The Grant tanks proved to be impossible to knock out except at close range.[161]

Renewing the attack on the morning of 28 May, Rommel concentrated on encircling and destroying separate units of the British armour. Repeated British counterattacks threatened to cut off and destroy the Afrika Korps. Running low on fuel, Rommel assumed a defensive posture, forming "the Cauldron". He made use of the extensive British minefields to shield his western flank. Meanwhile, Italian infantry cleared a path through the mines to provide supplies. On 30 May Rommel resumed the offensive, attacking westwards to link with elements of Italian X Corps, which had cleared a path through the Allied minefields to establish a supply line.[162] On 1 June, Rommel accepted the surrender of some 3,000 soldiers of the 150th Brigade.[163] On 6 June, 90th Light Division and the *Trieste* Division assaulted the Free French strongpoint in the Battle of Bir Hakeim, but the defenders continued to thwart the attack until finally evacuating on 10 June.[164] With his communications and the southern strongpoint of the British line thus secured, Rommel shifted his attack north again, relying on the British minefields of the Gazala lines to protect his left flank.[165] Threatened with being completely cut off, the British began a retreat eastward toward Egypt on 14 June, the so-called "Gazala Gallop."[166]

On 15 June Axis forces reached the coast, cutting off the escape for the Commonwealth forces still occupying the Gazala positions. With this task completed, Rommel struck for Tobruk while the enemy was still confused and disorganised.[167] Tobruk's defenders were at this point the 2nd South African Infantry Division, 4th Antiaircraft Brigade, 11th Indian Infantry, 32nd Army Tank, and 201st Guards Brigades, all under command of Major General Hendrik Klopper. The assault on Tobruk began at dawn on 20 June, and Klopper surrendered at dawn the following day.[168] With Tobruk, Rommel achieved the capture of 32,000 defenders, the port, and huge quantities of supplies.[169] Only at the fall of Singapore, earlier that year, had more British Commonwealth troops been captured at one time. On 22 June, Hitler promoted Rommel to Generalfeldmarschall for this victory.[170,171]</ref>

Figure 14: *The Afrika Korps enters Tobruk.*

Figure 15: *Rommel in 1942*

Following his success at Gazala and Tobruk, Rommel wanted to seize the moment and not allow 8th Army a chance to regroup.[172] He strongly argued that the Panzerarmee should advance into Egypt and drive on to Alexandria and the Suez Canal, as this would place almost all the Mediterranean coastline in Axis hands, ease conditions on the Eastern Front, and potentially lead to the capture from the south of the oil fields in the Caucasus and Middle East.[173] Indeed, Allied strategists feared that if Rommel captured Egypt, he would next overrun the Middle East before possibly linking up with the forces besieging the Caucasus. However, Hitler viewed the North African campaign primarily as a way to assist his Italian allies, not as an objective in and of itself. He would not consider sending Rommel the reinforcements and supplies he needed to take and hold Egypt, as this would have required diverting men and supplies from his primary focus: the Eastern Front.[174]

Rommel's success at Tobruk worked against him, as Hitler no longer felt it was necessary to proceed with Operation Herkules, the proposed attack on Malta.[175] Auchinleck relieved Ritchie of command of the Eighth Army on 25 June, and temporarily took command himself.[176] Rommel knew that delay would only benefit the British, who continued to receive supplies at a faster rate than Rommel could hope to achieve. He pressed an attack on the heavily fortified town of Mersa Matruh, which Auchinleck had designated as the fall-back position, surrounding it on 28 June.[177] The 2nd New Zealand Division and 50th (Northumbrian) Infantry Division were almost caught, with 50th Division fleeing on the 27th and 2nd Division escaping after a short engagement during the pre-dawn hours of 28 June. The four divisions of X Corps were caught in the encirclement, and were ordered by Auchinleck to attempt a breakout. The 29th Indian Infantry Brigade was nearly destroyed, losing 6,000 troops and 40 tanks.[178] The fortress fell on 29 June. In addition to stockpiles of fuel and other supplies, the British abandoned hundreds of tanks and trucks. Those that were functional were put into service by the Panzerarmee.[179]

El Alamein

First Battle of El Alamein

July, 1942

Rommel continued his pursuit of the Eighth Army, which had fallen back to heavily prepared defensive positions at El Alamein. This region is a natural choke point, where the Qattara Depression creates a relatively short line to defend that could not be outflanked to the south because of the steep escarpment. On 1 July the First Battle of El Alamein began. Rommel had around 100 available tanks. The Allies were able to achieve local air superiority, with heavy bombers attacking the 15th and 21st Panzers, who had also been delayed by a sandstorm. The 90th Light Division veered off course and were

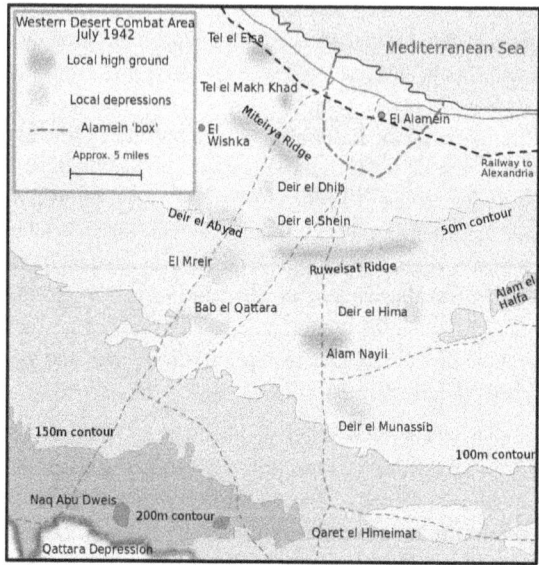

Figure 16: *El Alamein and surrounding area*

pinned down by South African artillery fire. Rommel continued to attempt to advance for two more days, but repeated sorties by the Desert Air Force meant he could make no progress.[180] On 3 July, he wrote in his diary that his strength had "faded away".[181] Attacks by 21st Panzer on 13 and 14 July were repulsed, and an Australian attack on 16–17 July was held off with difficulty.[182] Throughout the first half of July, Auchinleck concentrated attacks on the Italian 60th Infantry Division Sabratha at Tel el Eisa. The ridge was captured by the 26th Australian Brigade on 16 July.[183] Both sides suffered similar losses throughout the month, but the Axis supply situation remained less favourable. Rommel realised that the tide was turning.[184] A break in the action took place at the end of July as both sides rested and regrouped.[185]

Preparing for a renewed drive, the British replaced Auchinleck with General Harold Alexander on 8 August. Bernard Montgomery was made the new commander of Eighth Army that same day. The Eighth Army had initially been assigned to General William Gott, but he was killed when his plane was shot down on 7 August.[186] Rommel knew that a British convoy carrying over 100,000 tons of supplies was due to arrive in September.[187] He decided to launch an attack at the end of August with the 15th and 21st Panzer Division, 90th Light Division, and the Italian XX Motorized Corps in a drive through the southern flank of the El Alamein lines.[188] Expecting an attack sooner rather

Figure 17: *Rommel in a Sd.Kfz. 250/3*

than later, Montgomery fortified the Alam el Halfa ridge with the 44th Division, and positioned the 7th Armoured Division about 15 miles (24 km) to the south.[189]

Battle of Alam El Halfa

30 August - 5 September 1942

The Battle of Alam el Halfa was launched on 30 August. The terrain left Rommel with no choice but to follow a similar tactic as he had at previous battles: the bulk of the forces attempted to sweep around from the south while secondary attacks were launched on the remainder of the front. It took much longer than anticipated to get through the minefields in the southern sector, and the tanks got bogged down in unexpected patches of quicksand (Montgomery had arranged for Rommel to acquire a falsified map of the terrain).[190,191] Under heavy fire from British artillery and aircraft, and in the face of well prepared positions that Rommel could not hope to outflank due to lack of fuel, the attack stalled. By 2 September, Rommel realized the battle was unwinnable, and decided to withdraw.[192]

Montgomery had made preparations to cut the Germans off in their retreat, but in the afternoon of 2 September he visited Corps commander Brian Horrocks and gave orders to allow the Germans to retire. This was to preserve his own strength intact for the main battle which was to come.[193] On the

Figure 18: *Destroyed Panzer IIIs at Tel el Eisa, near El Alamein (1942)*

night of 3 September the 2nd New Zealand Division and 7th Armoured Division positioned to the north engaged in an assault, but they were repelled in a fierce rearguard action by the 90th Light Division. Montgomery called off further action to preserve his strength and allow for further desert training for his forces.[194] In the attack Rommel had suffered 2,940 casualties and lost 50 tanks, a similar number of guns, and 400 lorries, vital for supplies and movement. The British losses, except tank losses of 68, were much less, further adding to the numerical inferiority of Panzer Army Afrika. The Desert Air Force inflicted the highest proportions of damage on Rommel's forces. He now realized the war in Africa could not be won.[195] Physically exhausted and suffering from a liver infection and low blood pressure, Rommel flew home to Germany to recover his health.[196,197] General Georg Stumme was left in command in Rommel's absence.[187]

Second Battle of El Alamein

23 October–11 November 1942

Improved decoding by British intelligence (see Ultra) meant that the Allies had advance knowledge of virtually every Mediterranean convoy, and only 30 per cent of shipments were getting through.[198] In addition, Mussolini diverted supplies intended for the front to his garrison at Tripoli, and refused to release any additional troops to Rommel.[199] The increasing Allied air superiority and lack of fuel meant Rommel was forced to take a more defensive posture than he would have liked for the second Battle of El Alamein.[200] The German defences to the west of the town included a minefield 5 miles (8 km) deep with the main defensive line – itself several thousand yards deep – to its west.[201] This, Rommel hoped, would allow his infantry to hold the line at any

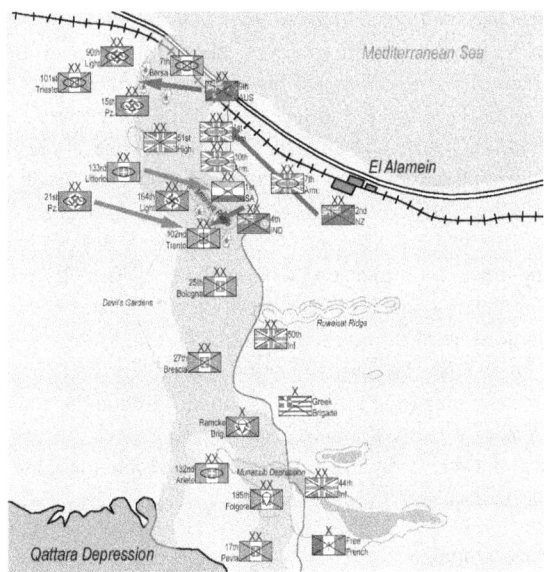

Figure 19: *Second Battle of El Alamein. Situation on 28 October 1942*

point until motorized and armoured units in reserve could move up and counterattack any Allied breaches.[202] The British offensive began on 23 October. Stumme, in command in Rommel's absence, died of an apparent heart attack while examining the front on 24 October, and Rommel was ordered to return from his medical leave, arriving on the 25th.[203] Montgomery's intention was to clear a narrow path through the minefield at the northern part of the defenses, at the area called Kidney Ridge, with a feint to the south. By the end of 25 October, 15th Panzers, the defenders in this sector, had only 31 serviceable tanks remaining of their initial force of 119.[204] Rommel brought the 21st Panzer and Ariete Divisions north on 26 October, to bolster the sector. On the 28th, Montgomery shifted his focus to the coast, ordering his 1st and 10th Armoured Divisions to attempt to swing around and cut off Rommel's line of retreat. Meanwhile, Rommel concentrated his attack on the Allied salient at Kidney Ridge, inflicting heavy losses. However, Rommel had only 150 operational tanks remaining, and Montgomery had 800, many of them Shermans.[205]

Montgomery, seeing his armoured brigades losing tanks at an alarming rate, stopped major attacks until the early hours of 2 November, when he opened Operation Supercharge, with a massive artillery barrage.[206] This was followed by penetration at the salient by two armoured and two infantry divisions.[207] Rommel's counterattack at 11:00 inflicted severe casualties on the Commonwealth troops, but by 20:00, with only 35 tanks remaining, he ordered his forces to disengage and begin to withdraw.[208] At midnight, he informed the OKW of his decision, and received a reply directly from Hitler the following afternoon: he ordered Rommel and his troops to hold their position to the last man. Rommel, who believed that the lives of his soldiers should never be squandered needlessly, was stunned.[209] While he (like all members of the Wehrmacht) had pledged an oath of absolute obedience to Hitler, he thought this order was pointless, even madness, and had to be disobeyed.[210] Rommel initially complied with the order, but after discussions with Kesselring and others, he issued orders for a retreat on 4 November.[211] The delay proved costly in terms of his ability to get his forces out of Egypt. He later said the decision to delay was what he most regretted from his time in Africa.[212] Meanwhile, the British 1st and 7th Armoured Division had broken through the German defences and were preparing to swing north and surround the Axis forces.[213] On the evening of the 4th, Rommel finally received word from Hitler authorizing the withdrawal.[214] By this time it was impossible for Rommel to save his non-motorized units.[215,216]

End of Africa campaign

Retreat across Africa

As Rommel attempted to withdraw his forces before the British could cut off his retreat, he fought a series of delaying actions. Heavy rains slowed movements and grounded the Desert Air Force, which aided the withdrawal. Those parts of Panzerarmee Africa that were motorized slipped away from El Alamein, but were under pressure from the pursuing Eighth Army. A series of short delaying actions was fought over the coastal highway, but no line could be held for any length of time, as Rommel lacked the armour and fuel to defend his open southern flank.[217] Rommel continued to retreat west, abandoning Halfaya Pass, Sollum, Mersa Brega and El Agheila.[218] The line Rommel was aiming for was 'Gabes gap' in Tunisia.[219] Luftwaffe Field Marshal Kesselring strongly criticized Rommel's decision to retreat all the way to Tunisia, as each airfield the Germans abandoned extended the range of the Allied bombers and fighters. Rommel defended his decision, pointing out that if he tried to assume a defensive position the Allies would destroy his forces and take the airfields anyway; the retreat saved the lives of his remaining men and shortened his supply lines. By now, Rommel's remaining forces fought in reduced strength combat groups, whereas the Allied forces had great numerical superiority and control of the air. Upon his arrival in Tunisia, Rommel noted with some bitterness the reinforcements, including the 10th Panzer Division, arriving in Tunisia following the Allied invasion of Morocco.[220]

Figure 20: *Rommel speaks with troops who are using a captured American M3 half-track, Tunisia.*

Tunisia

Having reached Tunisia, Rommel launched an attack against the U.S. II Corps which was threatening to cut his lines of supply north to Tunis. Rommel inflicted a sharp defeat on the American forces at the Kasserine Pass in February, his last battlefield victory of the war, and his first engagement against the United States Army.[221]

Rommel immediately turned back against the British forces, occupying the Mareth Line (old French defences on the Libyan border). While Rommel was at Kasserine at the end of January 1943, the Italian General Giovanni Messe was appointed commander of Panzer Army Africa, renamed the Italo-German Panzer Army in recognition of the fact that it consisted of one German and three Italian corps. Though Messe replaced Rommel, he diplomatically deferred to him, and the two coexisted in what was theoretically the same command. On 23 February *Armeegruppe Afrika* was created with Rommel in command. It included the Italo-German Panzer Army under Messe (renamed 1st Italian Army) and the German 5th Panzer Army in the north of Tunisia under General Hans-Jürgen von Arnim.

The last Rommel offensive in North Africa was on 6 March 1943, when he attacked Eighth Army at the Battle of Medenine.[222] The attack was made with

10th, 15th, and 21st Panzer Divisions. Alerted by Ultra intercepts, Montgomery deployed large numbers of anti-tank guns in the path of the offensive. After losing 52 tanks, Rommel called off the assault.[223] On 9 March he returned to Germany.[224] Command was handed over to General Hans-Jürgen von Arnim. Rommel never returned to Africa.[225] The fighting there continued on for another two months, until 13 May 1943, when General Messe surrendered the *Armeegruppe Afrika* to the Allies.

Italy 1943

On 23 July 1943 Rommel was moved to Greece as commander of Army Group E to counter a possible British invasion of the Greek coast. He arrived in Greece on 25 July but was recalled to Berlin the same date due to the overthrow of Mussolini. Rommel was to be posted to Italy as commander of the newly formed Army Group B. On 16 August 1943 Rommel's headquarters moved to Lake Garda in northern Italy and formally assumed command of the army group, which consisted of the 44th Infantry Division, the 26th Panzer Division and the 1st SS Panzer Division Leibstandarte SS Adolf Hitler. When Italy announced armistice with the Allies on 8 September, his forces took part in Operation Achse, disarming the Italian forces.[226]

Hitler met with Rommel and Kesselring to discuss future operations in Italy on 30 September 1943. Rommel insisted on a defensive line north of Rome, while Kesselring was more optimistic and advocated holding a line south of Rome. Hitler preferred Kesselring's appreciation and therefore revoked his prior decision for a subsequent subordination of Kesselring's forces to Rommel's army group. On 19 October Hitler decided that Kesselring would be the overall commander of the forces in Italy, sidelining Rommel.[227]

Rommel had wrongly predicted that the collapse of the German line in Italy would be fast. On 21 November Hitler gave Kesselring overall command of the Italian theater, moving Rommel and Army Group B to Normandy in France with responsibility for defending the French coast against the long anticipated Allied invasion.[228]

Atlantic Wall 1944

There was broad disagreement in the German High Command as to how best to meet the expected allied invasion of Northern France. The Commander-in-Chief West, Gerd von Rundstedt, believed there was no way to stop the invasion near the beaches due to the firepower possessed by the Allied navies, as had been experienced at Salerno.[229] He argued that the German armour should be held in reserve well inland near Paris where they could be used to counter-attack in force in a more traditional military doctrine. The allies could

Figure 21: *Rommel observes the fall of shot at Riva-Bella, just north of Caen in the area that would become Sword Beach in Normandy.*

be allowed to extend themselves deep into France where a battle for control would be fought, allowing the Germans to envelop the allied forces in a pincer movement, cutting off their avenue of retreat. He feared the piecemeal commitment of their armoured forces would cause them to become caught in a battle of attrition which they could not hope to win.[229]

The notion of holding the armour inland to use as a mobile reserve force from which they could mount a powerful counterattack applied the classic use of armoured formations as seen in France 1940. These tactics were still effective on the Eastern Front, where control of the air was important but did not dominate the action. Rommel's own experiences at the end of the North African campaign revealed to him that the Germans would not be allowed to preserve their armour from air attack for this type of massed assault.[229] Rommel believed their only opportunity would be to oppose the landings directly at the beaches, and to counterattack there before the invaders could become well established. Though there had been some defensive positions established and gun emplacements made, the Atlantic Wall was a token defensive line. Rundstedt had confided to Rommel that it was for propaganda purposes only.[230]

Upon arriving in Northern France Rommel was dismayed by the lack of completed works. According to Ruge, Rommel was in a staff position and could not issue orders, but he took every effort to explain his plan to commanders down to the platoon level, who took up his words eagerly, but "more or less open" opposition from the above slowed down the process. Finally, Rundstedt, who

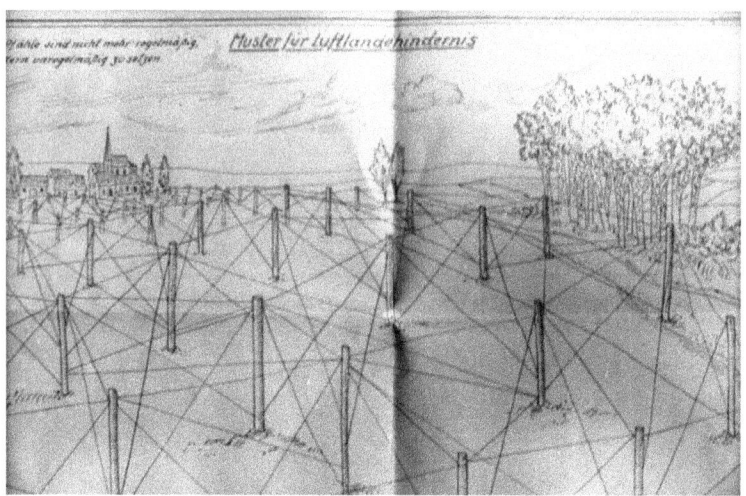

Figure 22: *A sketch by Rommel. His words on the picture: "Patterns for anti-airlanding obstacles. Now to be spaced irregularly instead of regularly". The House of Local History of Baden-Württemberg now keeps several of these, some hand-coloured by Rommel himself.*[6]

only respected Rommel grudgingly (he called him Field Marshal Cub),[231,232] intervened and supported Rommel's request for being made a commander.[233] It was granted in January or February 1944, when "much valuable time had been lost." He set out to improve the fortifications along the Atlantic Wall with great energy and engineering skill.[234]</ref>[235]</ref>[236]</ref>[237]</ref>. He had millions of mines laid and thousands of tank traps and obstacles set up on the beaches and throughout the countryside, including in fields suitable for glider aircraft landings, the so-called Rommel's asparagus.[238] (The Allies would later counter these with Hobart's Funnies)[239] In April 1944 Rommel promised Hitler that the preparations would be complete by 1 May, but by the time of the Allied invasion the preparations were far from finished. The quality of some of the troops manning them was poor and many bunkers lacked sufficient stocks of ammunition.[238]

Rundstedt expected the Allies to invade in the Pas-de-Calais because it was the shortest crossing point from Britain, its port facilities were essential to supplying a large invasion force, and the distance from Calais to Germany was relatively short.[240] Rommel and Hitler's views on the matter is a matter of debate between authors, with both seeming to change their positions.

Hitler vacillated between the two strategies. In late April, he ordered the I SS Panzer Corps placed near Paris, far enough inland to be useless to Rommel,

Figure 23: *Inspecting 21st Panzer Division troops and a mule track carrier of the Nebelwerfer.*

but not far enough for Rundstedt. Rommel moved those armoured formations under his command as far forward as possible, ordering General Erich Marcks, commanding the 84th Corps defending the Normandy section, to move his reserves into the frontline. Although Rommel was the dominating personality in Normandy with Rundstedt willing to delegate most of the responsibilities to him (the central reserve was Rundstedt's idea but he did not oppose to some form of coastal defense, and gradually came under the influence of Rommel's thinking), Rommel's strategy of an armor-supported coastal defense line was opposed by some officers, most notably Leo Geyr von Schweppenburg, who was supported by Guderian.[241,229] Hitler compromised and gave Rommel three divisions (the 2nd, the 21st and the 116th Panzer), let Rundstedt retain four and turned the other three to Army Group G, pleasing no one.[242]

The Allies staged elaborate deceptions for D-Day (see Operation Fortitude), giving the impression that the landings would be at Calais. Although Hitler himself expected a Normandy invasion for a while, Rommel and most Army commanders in France believed there would be two invasions, with the main invasion coming at the Pas-de-Calais. Rommel drove defensive preparations all along the coast of Northern France, particularly concentrating fortification building in the River Somme estuary. By D-Day on 6 June 1944 nearly all the German staff officers, including Hitler's staff, believed that Pas-de-Calais was going to be the main invasion site, and continued to believe so even after the landings in Normandy had occurred.[243]

Figure 24: *Generalfeldmarschälle Gerd von Rundstedt and Erwin Rommel meeting in Paris.*

The 5 June storm in the channel seemed to make a landing very unlikely, and a number of the senior officers were away from their units for training exercises and various other efforts. On 4 June the chief meteorologist of the 3 Air Fleet reported that weather in the channel was so poor there could be no landing attempted for two weeks. On 5 June Rommel left France and on 6 June he was at home celebrating his wife's birthday.[238] He was recalled and returned to his headquarters at 10 pm. Meanwhile, earlier in the day, Rundstedt had requested the reserves be transferred to his command. At 10 am Keitel advised that Hitler declined to release the reserves but that Rundstedt could move the 12th SS Panzer Division Hitlerjugend closer to the coast, with the Panzer-Lehr-Division placed on standby. Later in the day, Rundstedt received authorisation to move additional units in preparation for a counterattack, which Rundstedt decided to launch on 7 June. Upon arrival, Rommel concurred with the plan. By nightfall, Rundstedt, Rommel and Speidel continued to believe that the Normandy landing might have been a diversionary attack, as the Allied deception measures still pointed towards Calais. The 7 June counterattack did not take place as the 12th SS did not arrive on time due to the Allied air bombardments.[244] All this made the German command structure in France in disarray during the opening hours of the D-Day invasion.[245]

Facing relatively small-scale German counterattacks, the Allies secured five beachheads by nightfall of 6 June, landing 155,000 troops.[246] The Allies pushed ashore and expanded their beachhead despite strong German resistance. Rommel believed that if his armies pulled out of range of Allied naval fire, it would give them a chance to regroup and re-engage them later with a better chance of success. While he managed to convince Rundstedt, they still needed to win over Hitler. At a meeting with Hitler in Margival on 17 June, Rommel warned Hitler about the inevitable collapse in the German defences, but was rebuffed and told to focus on military operations.[247,248]

By mid-July the German position was crumbling. On 17 July 1944, Rommel was returning from visiting the headquarters of the I SS Panzer Corps. According to a widely accepted version of events, an RCAF Spitfire of 412 Squadron piloted by Charley Fox strafed his staff car near Sainte-Foy-de-Montgommery. The driver sped up and attempted to get off the main roadway, but a 20 mm round shattered his left arm, causing the vehicle to veer off of the road and crash into trees. Rommel was thrown from the car, suffering injuries to the left side of his face from glass shards and three fractures to his skull.[249] He was hospitalised with major head injuries (assumed to be almost certainly fatal).[250]

Plot against Hitler

The role that Rommel played in the military's resistance against Hitler or the 20 July plot is difficult to ascertain, as people most directly involved did not survive and limited documentation on the conspirators' plans and preparations exists.[251,252] The strongest evidence that points to the possibility that Rommel came to support the assassination plan was General Eberbach's confession to his son (eavesdropped by British agencies) while in British captivity, which stated that Rommel explicitly said to him that Hitler and his close associates had to be killed because this would be the only way out for Germany. This conversation occurred about a month before Rommel was coerced into committing suicide. Other notable evidence includes the papers of Rudolf Hartmann, one of the surviving leaders of the military resistance (alongside General Hans Speidel, Colonel Karl-Richard Kossmann, Colonel Eberhard Finckh and Lieutenant Colonel Caesar von Hofacker). These papers, accidentally discovered by historian Christian Schweizer in 2018 while doing research on Rudolf Hartmann, include Hartmann's eyewitness account of a conversation between Rommel and Carl-Heinrich von Stülpnagel in May 1944, as well as photos of the mid-May 1944 meeting between the inner circle of the resistance and Rommel at Kossmann's house. According to Hartmann, by the end of May, in another meeting at Hartmann's quarters in Mareil-Marly, Rommel showed "decisive determination" and clear approval of the inner circle's plan.

According to a post-war account by Karl Strölin, three of Rommel's friends—the *Oberbürgermeister* of Stuttgart, Strölin (who had served with

Figure 25: *Bomb blast damage following attempt to kill Hitler on 20 July 1944*

Rommel in the First World War), Alexander von Falkenhausen and Carl Heinrich von Stülpnagel—began efforts to bring Rommel into the anti-Hitler conspiracy in early 1944. According to Strölin, sometime in February, Rommel agreed to lend his support to the resistance.[253] On 15 April 1944 Rommel's new chief of staff, Hans Speidel, arrived in Normandy and reintroduced Rommel to Stülpnagel.[254] Speidel had previously been connected to Carl Goerdeler, the civilian leader of the resistance, but not to the plotters led by Claus von Stauffenberg, and came to Stauffenberg's attention only due to his appointment to Rommel's headquarters. The conspirators felt they needed the support of a field marshal on active duty. Erwin von Witzleben, who would have become commander-in-chief of the Wehrmacht had the plot succeeded, was a field marshal, but had been inactive since 1942. The conspirators gave instructions to Speidel to bring Rommel into their circle.[255]

Speidel met with former foreign minister Konstantin von Neurath and Strölin on 27 May in Germany, ostensibly at Rommel's request, although the latter was not present. Neurath and Strölin suggested opening immediate surrender negotiations in the West, and, according to Speidel, Rommel agreed to further discussions and preparations.[248] Around the same timeframe, the plotters in Berlin were not aware that Rommel had allegedly decided to take part in the conspiracy. On 16 May, they informed Allen Dulles, through whom they hoped to negotiate with the Western Allies, that Rommel could not be counted on for support.[256]

At least initially, Rommel opposed assassinating Hitler.[257] According to some authors,[258,259] he gradually changed his attitude. After the war, his widow—among others—maintained that Rommel believed an assassination attempt would spark civil war in Germany and Austria, and Hitler would have become a martyr for a lasting cause.[260] Instead, Rommel reportedly suggested that Hitler be arrested and brought to trial for his crimes; he did not attempt to implement this plan when Hitler visited Margival, France, on 17 June. The arrest plan would have been highly improbable, as Hitler's security was extremely tight. Rommel would have known this, having commanded Hitler's army protection detail in 1939.[261] He was in favour of peace negotiations, and repeatedly urged Hitler to negotiate with the Allies, which is dubbed by some as "hopelessly naive", considering no one would trust Hitler,[262,3] and "as naive as it was idealistic, the attitude he showed to the man he had sworn loyalty".[263] On 15 July, Rommel wrote a letter to Hitler giving him a "last chance" to end the hostilities with the Western Allies, urging Hitler to "draw the proper conclusions without delay." What Rommel didn't know was that the letter took two weeks to reach Hitler because of Kluge's precautions.[264] Various authors report that many German generals in Normandy, including some SS officers like Hausser, Bittrich, Dietrich (a hard-core Nazi and Hitler's long-time supporter) and Rommel's former opponent Geyr von Schweppenburg pledged support to him, even against Hitler's orders, while Kluge supported him with much hesitation.[251] Von Rundstedt encouraged Rommel to carry out his plans but refused to do anything himself, remarking that it had to be a man who was still young and loved by the people, while von Manstein was also approached by Rommel but categorically refused, although he did not report them to Hitler either.

On 17 July Rommel was incapacitated by an Allied air attack, which many authors describe as a fateful event that drastically altered the outcome of the bomb plot.[265,266] Writer Ernst Jünger commented: "The blow that felled Rommel ... robbed the plan of the shoulders that were to be entrusted the double weight of war and civil war - the only man who had enough naivety to counter the simple terror that those he was about to go against possessed."[267]

After the failed bomb attack of 20 July, many conspirators were arrested and the dragnet expanded to thousands.[268] Rommel was first implicated when Stülpnagel, after his failed suicide attempt, repeatedly muttered "Rommel" in delirium. Under torture, Hofacker named Rommel as one of the participants.[269] Additionally, Goerdeler had written down Rommel's name on a list as potential Reich President (according to Stroelin, they had not managed to announce this intention to Rommel yet and he probably never heard of it until the end of his life).[270,271,272] On 27 September, Martin Bormann submitted to Hitler a memorandum which claimed that "the late General Stülpnagel,

Figure 26: *Rommel's funeral procession.*

Colonel von Hofacker, Kluge's nephew who has been executed, Lieutenant Colonel Rathgens, and several ... living defendants have testified that Field Marshal Rommel was perfectly in the picture about the assassination plan and has promised to be at the disposal of the New Government."[273] Gestapo agents were sent to Rommel's house in Ulm and placed him under surveillance.[274]

Death

Rommel's case was turned over to the "Court of Military Honour"—a drumhead court-martial convened to decide the fate of officers involved in the conspiracy. The court included, among others, Wilhelm Keitel, Heinz Guderian, Gerd von Rundstedt and Heinrich Kirchheim[275,276] (whom Rommel had fired after Tobruk in 1941).[131] The Court acquired information from Speidel, Hofacker and others that implicated Rommel, with Keitel and Kaltenbrunner assuming that he had taken part in the subversion. Keitel and Guderian then made the decision that favoured Speidel's case and at the same time shifted the blame to Rommel.[277,278,279] By normal procedure, this would lead to Rommel's being brought to Roland Freisler's People's Court, a kangaroo court that always decided in favour of the prosecution. However, Hitler knew that having Rommel branded and executed as a traitor would severely damage morale on the home front.[275] He thus decided to offer Rommel the chance to take his own life.[280]

Two generals from Hitler's headquarters, Wilhelm Burgdorf and Ernst Maisel, visited Rommel at his home on 14 October 1944. Burgdorf informed him of the charges and offered him three options: he could choose to defend himself personally to Hitler in Berlin,[281]</ref> or if he refused to do so (which would be taken as an admission of guilt), he would either face the People's Court—which would have been tantamount to a death sentence—or choose a quiet suicide. In the former case, his family would have suffered even before the all-but-certain conviction and execution, and his staff would have been arrested and executed as well. In the latter case, the government would claim that he died a hero and bury him with full military honours, and his family would receive full pension payments. Burgdorf had brought a cyanide capsule.[282]

Rommel denied involvement in the plot, declared his love for Hitler and that he would gladly serve his "Fatherland" again.[283] *Der Spiegel* takes notice of the fact that he was talking to his messengers of death and some would claim that he was acting out of helpless defense (although *Der Spiegel* thought his love for Hitler felt sincere)[284] while Remy suggests that Rommel was trying in some way to apologize to Hitler, towards whom he had conflicting emotions, which Ernst Maisel[285] realized and found "disgusting" and "a hypocrisy", because Maisel (a loyal, unapologetic Hitler supporter, even after the war) could not understand how someone could try to kill someone he loved (Rommel's previous replies about his role in the attempt made Maisel believe that he was part of the plot).[286,287,288,289]

As Rommel thought the matter over, an SS detachment surrounded his village, leading him to conclude that if he agreed to face the People's Court, he would not reach Berlin alive.[290] With that in mind, Rommel opted to commit suicide, and explained his decision to his wife and son.[290] Wearing his Afrika Korps jacket and carrying his field marshal's baton, Rommel went to Burgdorf's Opel, driven by SS Master Sergeant Heinrich Doose, and was driven out of the village. After stopping, Doose and Maisel walked away from the car, leaving Rommel with Burgdorf. Five minutes later Burgdorf gestured to the two men to return to the car, and Doose noticed that Rommel was slumped over, having taken the cyanide. He died before being taken to the Wagner-Schule field hospital. Ten minutes later, the group telephoned Rommel's wife to inform her of his death.[291,292,293,294] Witnesses were struck by the smile of deep contempt on the dead man's face, never seen in life, and his widow thought it was for Hitler.[295,296]

The official story of Rommel's death, as reported to the public, stated that Rommel had died of either a heart attack or a cerebral embolism—a complication of the skull fractures he had suffered in the earlier strafing of his staff car.[297,298,299] To strengthen the story still further, Hitler ordered an official day of mourning in commemoration. As previously promised, Rommel was given

Figure 27: *Rommel's grave*

a state funeral. The fact that his state funeral was held in Ulm instead of Berlin had, according to his son, been stipulated by Rommel.[300] Rommel had specified that no political paraphernalia be displayed on his corpse, but the Nazis made sure his coffin was festooned with swastikas. Hitler sent Field Marshal von Rundstedt, who was unaware that Rommel had died as a result of Hitler's orders, as his representative at Rommel's funeral.[301] The body was cremated so no incriminating evidence would be left.[295] The truth behind Rommel's death became known to the Allies when intelligence officer Charles Marshall interviewed Rommel's widow, Lucia Rommel,[302] as well as from a letter by Rommel's son Manfred in April 1945.

Rommel's grave is located in Herrlingen, a short distance west of Ulm. For decades after the war on the anniversary of his death, veterans of the Africa campaign, including former opponents, would gather at his tomb in Herrlingen.

Rommel's style as military commander

Rommel's experiences on the Italian front in the First World War which gained successes against opponents shaped Rommel's subsequent style as a military commander. Rommel was a successful tactician in a rapidly developing, mobile battle. He learned that taking initiative and not allowing the enemy forces to regroup led to victory. Some authors, like Porch, comment that Rommel's

Figure 28: *Rommel helping to free up his staff car, Škoda Superb Kfz 21*

enemies were often less organized, second-rate, or depleted, and his tactics were less effective against adequately led, trained and supplied opponents, and proved insufficient in the latter years of the war.[303] Others point out that through his career, he frequently fought while out-numbered and out-gunned, sometimes overwhelmingly so, while having to deal with internal opponents in Germany who hoped that he would fail.[304,305,306,307]

Rommel is praised by numerous authors as a great leader of men.[308]</ref>[309,310,311,312,313,314,315] The historian and journalist Basil Liddell Hart concludes that he was a strong leader who was worshipped by his troops and respected by his adversaries, and is deserving to be named as one of the "Great Captains of History."[316] Owen Connelly concurred, writing that "No better exemplar of military leadership can be found than Erwin Rommel", quoting Mellenthin on the inexplicable mutual understanding that existed between Rommel and his troops. Hitler, though, remarked that, "Unfortunately Field-Marshal Rommel is a very great leader full of drive in times of success, but an absolute pessimist when he meets the slightest problems."[317] Telp criticised Rommel for not extending the benevolence he showed in promoting his own officers' careers to his peers, who he ignored or slighted in his reports.[318]

Rommel received both praise and criticism for his leadership during the French campaign. Many, such as General Georg Stumme, who had previously commanded 7th Panzer Division, were impressed with the speed and success of Rommel's drive.[319] Others were reserved or critical: Kluge, the commanding officer, argued that Rommel's decisions were impulsive and that he claimed too much credit, by falsifying diagrams or not acknowledging contributions of other units, especially the Luftwaffe. Some pointed out that Rommel's division took the highest casualties in the campaign.[320] Others point out that in exchange for 2,160 casualties and 42 tanks, it captured more than 100,000 prisoners and destroyed nearly two divisions' worth of enemy tanks (about 450 tanks), vehicles and guns.[321,322]

Taking his opponents by surprise and creating uncertainty in their minds were key elements in Rommel's approach to offensive warfare: he took advantage of sand storms and the dark of night to conceal the movement of his forces.[323] Rommel was aggressive, often directed battle from the front or piloted a reconnaissance aircraft over the lines to get a view of the situation. When the British mounted a commando raid deep behind German lines in an effort to kill Rommel and his staff on the eve of their Crusader offensive, Rommel was indignant that the British expected to find his headquarters 250 miles behind his front.[324] Friedrich von Mellenthin and Harald Kuhn write that at times in North Africa his absence from a position of communication made command of the battles of the Afrika Korps difficult. Mellenthin lists Rommel's counterattack during Operation Crusader as one such instance.[325] Butler concurred, saying that leading from the front is a good concept, however Rommel took it so far (he frequently directed the actions of a single company or battalion) that he made communication and coordination between units problematic, as well as risking of life to where he could have been easily killed even by one of his own artillery batteries.[84] Kesselring also complained about Rommel cruising about the battlefield like a division or corps commander, but Gause and Westphal supported Rommel and replied that in the African desert only this method would work, and that it was useless to try to restrain Rommel anyway.[326] His staff officers, although admiring towards their leader, complained about the self-destructive Spartan lifestyle that made life harder, diminished his effectiveness and forced them to "babi[ed] him as unobstrusively as possible."[327,328,329]

Rommel spoke German with a pronounced southern German or Swabian accent. He was not a part of the Prussian aristocracy that dominated the German high command, and as such was looked upon somewhat suspiciously by the Wehrmacht's traditional power structure.[330,331] Rommel felt a commander should be physically more robust than the troops he led, and should always show them an example.[332,333] </ref> He expected his subordinate commanders to do the same.

Figure 29: *Rommel with German and Italian officers, 1942*

Rommel was direct, unbending, tough in his manners, to superiors and subordinates alike, disobedient even to Hitler whenever he saw fit, although he was gentle and diplomatic to the lower ranks (German and Italian alike) and POWs.[334,335] Despite being publicity-friendly, he was also shy, introverted, clumsy and overly formal even to his closest aides, judging people only on their merits, although loyal and considerate to those who had proved reliability, and displayed a surprisingly passionate and devoted side to a very small few (including Hitler) with whom he had dropped down the seemingly impenetrable barriers (many of these traits seemed to manifest even at a very young age).[336].

Relations with Italian forces

Rommel's relationship with the Italian High Command in North Africa was generally poor. Although he was nominally subordinate to the Italians, he enjoyed a certain degree of autonomy from them; since he was directing their troops in battle as well as his own, this was bound to cause hostility among Italian commanders. Conversely, as the Italian command had control over the supplies of the forces in Africa, they resupplied Italian units preferentially, which was a source of resentment for Rommel and his staff.[337] Rommel's direct and abrasive manner did nothing to smooth these issues.[338,339,340]

While certainly much less proficient than Rommel in their leadership, aggressiveness, tactical outlook and mobile warfare skills, Italian commanders were competent in logistics, strategy and artillery doctrine: their troops were ill-equipped but well-trained. As such, the Italian commanders were repeatedly at odds with Rommel over concerns with issues of supply.[341] Field Marshal Kesselring was assigned Supreme Commander Mediterranean, at least in part to alleviate command problems between Rommel and the Italians. This effort resulted only in partial success, with Kesselring's own relationship with the Italians being unsteady and Kesselring claiming Rommel ignored him as easily as he ignored the Italians.[342] Rommel often went directly to Hitler with his needs and concerns, taking advantage of the favoritism that the Führer displayed towards him and adding to the distrust that Kesselring and the German High Command already had of him.[343]

Very different, however, was the perception of Rommel by Italian common soldiers and NCOs, who, like the German field troops, had the deepest trust and respect for him.[344,345]</ref> Paolo Colacicchi, an officer in the Italian Tenth Army recalled that Rommel "became sort of a myth to the Italian soldiers" and that the Bersaglieri baptised him "Rommelito"(perhaps also a reference to both men's small stature: "Rommelito" means "little Rommel" while Romulus means "the little boy from Rome". Incidentally, Palestine Jews associated Rommel with Romulus as well, based on Ohr Hachaim's 200-year-old commentary on the account of Jacob wrestling with the angel). Rommel himself held a much more generous view about the Italian soldier[346] than about their leadership (towards whom his disdain, deeply rooted in militarism, was not atypical, although unlike Kesselring, he was incapable of concealing it) Unlike many of his superiors and subordinates who held racist views, he was usually "kindly disposed" to the Italians in general.

Some authors like Sadkovich blame Rommel for abandoning his Italian units, refusing cooperation, rarely acknowledging their achievements and other erroneous behaviours towards his Italian allies, while others point out that the Italians under Rommel, in comparison with many of their compatriots in other areas, were better led, supplied and trained, and fought well as a result, with a ratio of wounded and killed Italians similar to that of the Germans. In one case, a false accusation of Rommel's supposed mistreatment of Italians made by Goering was refuted by Mussolini himself.[347] In 1943, Jodl described Rommel as the only German commander numerous officers and soldiers in Italy would willingly subordinate to.[348]

Views on the conduct of war

Many authors describe Rommel as having a reputation of being a chivalrous, humane, and professional officer, and that he earned the respect of both his own troops and his enemies.[349,350,351] According to Young's biography and Luck's memoirs, during the desert campaign, interactions between German

Figure 30: *Rommel walks past Allied prisoners taken at Tobruk, 1942*

and British troops encountering each other between battles were sometimes openly friendly.[352,353] The same was not true in the Normandy Campaign, however, where both Allied and German troops murdered prisoners of war on occasion during June and July 1944.[354] According to Remy, although there were massacres caused by Hitler's orders (issued during Rommel's stay in a hospital), Rommel treated his Italian opponents with his usual fairness, requiring that the prisoners should be accorded the same conditions as German civilians. Remy opines that an order in which Rommel (who was actually protesting against Hitler's directives) called for no "sentimental scruples" against "Badoglio-dependent bandits in uniforms of the once brothers-in-arms" should not be taken out of context.[355] Peter Lieb agrees that the order did not radicalize the war and that the disarmament in Rommel's area of responsibility happened without major bloodshed.[356] Italian internees were sent to Germany for forced labour, but Rommel did not know about this.[355,356] In Normandy, Rommel withheld Hitler's Commando Order to execute captured commandos from Army Group B, with his units reporting that they were treating commandos as regular POWs. The same had most likely been done in North Africa,[357] however this is disputed by historian Szymon Datner who wrote that Rommel might have been simply trying to conceal atrocities of Nazi Germany from the Allies.[358] Other authors argue that generosity to opponents was a natural trait of the man, like Claus Telp who states that Rommel by nature was chivalrous and not prone to order needless violence,[359] or Robert Forczyk who considers Rommel a true great captain with chivalry. Maurice Remy states that due to the man's personality and some special circumstances, he was only really confronted with the reality of atrocities in 1944 (although he had heard rumours about massacres while fighting in Africa).[360] Some authors cite, among other cases, Rommel's naive reactions to what happened in Poland while being there: he paid a visit to his wife's uncle, famous Polish priest and patriotic leader Edmund Roszczynialski, who was murdered days after, which was never found out by Rommel who, at his wife's urgings, kept writing letter after letter to Himmler's adjutants asking them to keep track and take care of their relative.[361,362] Knopp and Mosier agree that he was naive politically, citing his request for a Jewish Gauleiter in 1943. Despite this, Peter Lieb finds it hard to believe that a man of Rommel's position could have known nothing about atrocities, although Lieb accepts that locally he was separated from places these atrocities happened, while *Der Spiegel* comments that Rommel was simply in denial about what happened around him.[6] Alaric Searle points out that it was the early diplomatic successes and bloodless expansion that blinded Rommel to the true nature of his beloved Führer, whom he kept naively supporting.[363] Scheck believes that it might be forever unclear whether Rommel recognized the unprecedented depraved character of the regime.[3] When Rommel learned about the atrocities *SS Division Leibstandarte* committed in Italy in September 1943, he allegedly forbade his son to join the Waffen-SS.[364]

Historian Richard J. Evans has stated that German soldiers in Tunisia raped Jewish women, and the success of Rommel's forces in capturing or securing Allied, Italian and Vichy French territory in North Africa led to many Jews in these areas being killed by other German institutions as part of the Holocaust.[365] Similarly, several German historians argued that while Rommel did not have strong racial views, if he had succeeded in his goal of invading the Middle East during 1942 large numbers of Jews in Palestine would have been murdered by an SS unit which had been deployed to North Africa in July 1942 to operate behind the lines of the Afrika Korps.[6] According to Mallmann and Cüppers, on 20 July, Walther Rauff, who was responsible for the unit, was sent to Tobruk to report to Rommel, however Rommel was 500 km away from Tobruk conducting the First El Alamein, so Mallmann and Cüppers found that the chance for a meeting between Rommel and Rauff (in which Rommel reportedly was disgusted after learning about the plan from Rauff and sent Rauff on his way), as described by a post-war CIA report, was hardly possible. On 29 July, Rauff's unit was sent to Athens, expecting to enter Africa when Rommel crossed the Nile. However, in view of the Axis' deteriorating situation in Africa, they returned to Germany in September. Historian Jean-Christoph Caron opines that there is no evidence that Rommel knew or would have supported Rauff's mission, and he also believes Rommel bore no direct responsibility regarding the SS's looting of gold in Tunisia. According to historian Haim Saadon, Director of the Center of Research on North African Jewry in WWII, there was no extermination plan: Rauff's documents show that his foremost concern was helping the Wehrmacht to win, and he came up with the idea of forced labour camps in the process.[366,367] By the time these labour camps were in effect, according to Ben Shepherd, Rommel had already been retreating and there is no proof of his contact with the Einsatzkommando.[368] Rommel had described the conduct of the desert war as "War without Hate" in his papers. Historian Martin Kitchen states that the reputation of the Afrika Korps was preserved due to circumstances: the sparsely populated desert areas did not lend themselves to ethnic cleansing; the German forces never reached Egypt and Palestine that had large Jewish populations; and in the urban areas of Tunisia and Tripolitania, the Italian government constrained the German efforts to discriminate against or eliminate Jews who were Italian citizens.[369] Despite this, the North African Jews themselves believed that it was Rommel who prevented the "Final Solution" from being carried out against them when German might dominated North Africa from Egypt to Morocco. According to Curtis and Remy, 120,000 Jews lived in Algeria, 200,000 in Morocco, about 80,000 in Tunisia (when the Germans invaded Tunisia in 1942, this number remained the same), 26,000 in Libya.[370] According to Marshall, he sharply protested the Jewish policies, other immoral activities and was an opponent of the Gestapo.[371] He also refused to comply with Hitler's order to execute Jewish POWs.[372,373] (His own Afrika Korps was known among soldiers of Jewish descent as a refuge, safe from racial laws and discrimination.) At his 17 June 1944 meeting with Hitler at Margival, he protested against the atrocity committed by the 2nd SS Panzer Division *Das Reich*, which had massacred the citizens of the French town of Oradour-sur-Glane. Rommel asked to be allowed to punish the division.[374] Building the Atlantic Wall was officially the responsibility of the Organisation Todt (which was not under Rommel's command), but he enthusiastically joined the task,[375] protesting slave labour and suggesting that they should recruit French civilians and pay them good wages.[376,377] Despite this, French civilians and Italian prisoners of war held by the Germans were forced by officials under the Vichy government, the Todt Organization and the SS forces[378] to work on building some of the defences Rommel ordered constructed, in appalling conditions according to historian Will Fowler. Although they got basic wages, the workers complained because it was too little and there was no heavy equipment.[379] Robin Neillands and Roderick De Normann report that German soldiers as well as Russian and Polish renegades were used to avoid forced labour. German troops also worked almost round-the-clock under very harsh conditions, with Rommel's rewards being accordions (Rommel was an eccentric and horrible violinist himself).[380] Lieb reports that he felt pity when he saw the French's suffering in his inspection tour and probably helped to save the lives of thousands of locals.[357]

Rick Atkinson criticizes Rommel for gaining a looted stamp collection (a bribe from Sepp Dietrich) and a villa taken from the Jews.[381] Lucas, Matthews and

Remy though describe the contemptuous and angry reaction of Rommel towards Dietrich's act, the lootings and other brutal behaviours of the SS that he had discovered in Italy.[382] Claudia Hecht also explains that although the Stuttgart and Ulm authorities did arrange for the Rommel family the brief use of a villa (whose Jewish owners had been forced out two years before that) after their house had been destroyed by Allied bombing, the ownership was never transferred to them.[383] Butler notes that Rommel was one of the few who refused large estates and gifts of cash Hitler gave to his generals.[384]

Curiously, a recent research by Norman Ohler claims that Rommel's behaviours were heavily influenced by Pervitin which he reportedly took in heavy doses, to such an extent that Ohler referred to him as "the Crystal Fox" ("Kristallfuchs") playing off the nickname "the Desert Fox" (a nickname famously given to him by the British, as reported by other sources).

In Nazi and Allied propaganda

At the beginning, although Hitler and Goebbels took particular notice of Rommel, the Nazi elites had no intent to create one major war symbol (partly out of fear that he would offset Hitler[385]), generating huge propaganda campaigns for not only Rommel but also Gerd von Rundstedt, Walther von Brauchitsch, Eduard Dietl, Sepp Dietrich (the latter two were party members and also strongly supported by Hitler), etc.[265] Despite this, due to a multitude of conditions such as Rommel's unusual charisma,[386] </ref>[387]</ref> his talents both in military matters and public relations[388,389]</ref> as well as no small help from Goebbels' propaganda machine and the Allies's participation in mythologizing his life (either for political benefits, sympathy for someone who evoked a romantic archetype,[390] or genuine admiration for his actions), the situation gradually developed to the point that, as Spiegel described, "Even back then his fame outshone that of all other commanders."

Rommel's victories in France were featured in the German press and in the February 1941 film *Victory in the West*, in which Rommel personally helped direct a segment reenacting the crossing of the Somme River.[391] Rommel's victories in 1941 were played up by the Nazi propaganda, even though his successes in North Africa were achieved in arguably one of Germany's least strategically important theaters of World War II.[87,392] In November 1941, Reich Minister of Propaganda Joseph Goebbels wrote about "the urgent need" to have Rommel "elevated to a kind of popular hero". Rommel, with his innate abilities as a military commander and love of the spotlight, was a perfect fit for the role Goebbels designed for him.[87]

Figure 31: *Rommel at a Paris victory parade (June 1940). Rommel had access to Reich Minister of Propaganda Joseph Goebbels via a senior propaganda official Karl Hanke, who served under Rommel during the 1940 campaign.*[393]

Successes in North Africa

In North Africa, Rommel received help in cultivating his image from Alfred Ingemar Berndt, a senior official at the Reich Propaganda Ministry who had volunteered for military service.[394] Seconded by Goebbels, Berndt was assigned to Rommel's staff and became one of his closest aides. Berndt often acted as liaison between Rommel, the Propaganda Ministry and the Führer Headquarters. He directed Rommel's photo shoots and filed radio dispatches describing the battles.[395,396]

In the spring of 1941, Rommel's name began to appear in the British media. In the autumn of 1941 and early winter of 1941/1942, he was mentioned in the British press almost daily. Toward the end of the year, the Reich propaganda machine also used Rommel's successes in Africa as a diversion from the Wehrmacht's challenging situation in the Soviet Union with the stall of Operation Barbarossa.[397,398,399]</ref> The American press soon began to take notice of Rommel as well, following the country's entry into the war on 11 December 1941, writing that "The British (...) admire him because he beat them and were surprised to have beaten in turn such a capable general". General Auchinleck distributed a directive to his commanders seeking to dispel the notion that Rommel was a "superman".⁴⁰⁰,⁴⁰¹ Rommel, no matter how hard the situation was, made a deliberate effort at always spending some time with soldiers and patients, his own and POWs alike, which contributed greatly to his reputation of not only being a great commander but also "a decent chap" among the troops.

The attention of the Western and especially the British press thrilled Goebbels, who wrote in his diary in early 1942: "Rommel continues to be the recognized darling of even the enemies' news agencies."⁴⁰² The Field Marshal was pleased by the media attention, although he knew the downsides of having a reputation.⁴⁰²,⁴⁰³</ref>⁴⁰⁴ Hitler took note of the British propaganda as well, commenting in the summer of 1942 that Britain's leaders must have hoped "to be able to explain their defeat to their own nation more easily by focusing on Rommel."⁴⁰⁵

The Field Marshal was the German commander most frequently covered in the German media, and the only one to be given a press conference, which took place in October 1942.³⁹⁶,⁴⁰⁶ The press conference was moderated by Goebbels and was attended by both domestic and foreign media. Rommel declared: "Today we (...) have the gates of Egypt in hand, and with the intent to act!" Keeping the focus on Rommel distracted the German public from Wehrmacht losses elsewhere as the tide of the war began to turn. He became a symbol that was used to reinforce the German public's faith in an ultimate Axis victory.⁴⁰⁷

Military reverses

In the wake of the successful British offensive in November 1942 and other military reverses, the Propaganda Ministry directed the media to emphasize Rommel's invincibility. The charade was maintained until the spring of 1943, even as the German situation in Africa became increasingly precarious. To ensure that the inevitable defeat in Africa would not be associated with Rommel's name, Goebbels had the Supreme High Command announce in May 1943 that Rommel was on a two-month leave for health reasons.⁴⁰⁸,⁴⁰⁹</ref> Instead, the campaign was presented, by Berndt, who resumed his role in the Propaganda Ministry, as a ruse to tie down the British Empire while Germany was turning Europe into an impenetrable fortress, with Rommel at the helm of this success. After the radio program ran in May 1943, Rommel sent Berndt a case of cigars as a sign of his gratitude.⁴⁰⁸

Although Rommel then entered a period without a significant command, he remained a household name in Germany, synonymous with the aura of invincibility.⁴¹⁰ Hitler then made Rommel part of his defensive strategy for Fortress Europe (*Festung Europa*) by sending him to the West to inspect fortifications

Figure 32: *One of the many propaganda photographs of Rommel on inspection tours of the Atlantic wall.*

along the Atlantic Wall. Goebbels supported the decision, noting in his diary that Rommel was "undoubtedly the suitable man" for the task. The propaganda minister expected the move to reassure the German public and at the same time to have a negative impact on the Allied forces' morale.[411]

In France, a Wehrmacht propaganda company frequently accompanied Rommel on his inspection trips to document his work for both domestic and foreign audiences.[412,413] In May 1944 the German newsreels reported on Rommel's speech at a Wehrmacht conference, where he stated his conviction that "every single German soldier will make his contribution against the Anglo-American spirit that it deserves for its criminal and bestial air war campaign against our homeland". The speech led to an upswing in morale and sustained confidence in Rommel.[414]

When Rommel was seriously wounded on 17 July 1944, the Propaganda Ministry undertook efforts to conceal the injury so as not to undermine domestic morale. Despite those, the news leaked to the British press. To counteract the rumors of a serious injury and even death, Rommel was required to appear at the 1 August press conference. On 3 August, the German press published an official report that Rommel had been injured in a car accident. Rommel noted in his diary his dismay at this twisting of the truth, belatedly realising how much the Reich propaganda was using him for its own ends.[414]

Rommel's views on propaganda

Rommel was interested in propaganda, beyond the promotion of his own image. In 1944, after visiting Rommel in France and reading his proposals on counteracting Allied propaganda, Alfred-Ingemar Berndt remarked: "He is also interested in this propaganda business and wants to develop it by all means. He has even thought and brought out practical suggestions for each program and subject."

Rommel saw the propaganda and education values in his and his nation's deeds (He also did value justice itself: According to Admiral Ruge's diary, Rommel told Ruge: "Justice is the indispensable foundation of a nation. Unfortunately the higher-ups are not clean. The slaughterings are grave sins."[415]) The key to the successful creating of an image, according to Rommel, was leading by example: "The men tend to feel no kind of contact with a commander who, they know, is sitting somewhere in headquarters. What they want is what might be termed a physical contact with him. In moments of panic, fatigue, or disorganization, or when something out of the ordinary has to be demanded from them, the personal example of the commander works wonders, especially if he has had the wit to create some sort of legend around himself."[416] He urged Axis authorities to treat the Arab with the utmost respect to prevent uprisings behind the front.

He protested the use of propaganda at the cost of explicit military benefits though.[417] Ruge suggests that his chief treated his own fame as a kind of weapon.

The political scientist and historian Randall Hansen suggests that Rommel chose his whole command style for the purpose of spreading meritocracy and egalitarianism, as well as Nazi ideals he shared with Hitler due to their common non-aristocratic background. His egalitarianism extended to people of other races:[418] in replying to white South African officers' demands that the black POWs should be housed in separated compounds, he refused, commenting that the black soldiers wore the same uniforms and had fought alongside the whites, and thus were their equals.[419] On the other hand, Watson comments that, regarding the Afrika Korps, any Nazi indoctrination was minimised, allowing Rommel the freedom to reinvent his army in his own style.[420] Rommel's proposals were not always practical: in 1943, he surprised Hitler by proposing that a Jew should be made into a Gauleiter to prove to the world that Germany was innocent of accusations that Rommel had heard from the enemy's propaganda regarding the mistreatment of Jews. Hitler replied "Dear Rommel, you understand nothing about my thinking at all".[6]

Figure 33: *Erwin Rommel and Adolf Hitler in 1942*

Relationship with National Socialism

Rommel was not a member of the Nazi Party.[421] Rommel and Hitler had a close and genuine, if complicated, personal relationship. Rommel, as other Wehrmacht officers, welcomed the Nazi rise to power.[422,61] Numerous historians state that Rommel was one of Hitler's favorite generals and that his close relationship with the dictator benefited both his inter-war and war-time career.[63,423,61] Robert Citino describes Rommel as "not apolitical" and writes that he owed his career to Hitler, to whom Rommel's attitude was "worshipful",[396] with Messenger agreeing that Rommel owed his tank command, his hero status and other promotions to Hitler's interference and support.[396,424,425] Peter Caddick-Adams: "As is now clear, Rommel had been very close to Hitler and the Third Reich ..."[426]</ref>

Kesselring described Rommel's own power over Hitler as "hypnotic". In 1944, Rommel himself told Ruge and his wife that Hitler had a kind of irresistible magnetic aura ("magnetismus") and was always seemingly in an intoxicated condition.[427] Maurice Remy identifies that the point at which their relationship became a personal one was 1939, when Rommel proudly announced to his friend Kurt Hesse that he had "sort of forced Hitler to go with me (to the Hradschin Castle in Prague, in an open top car, without another bodyguard), under my personal protection ... He had entrusted himself to me and would never forget me for my excellent advice."[428]

The close relationship between Rommel and Hitler continued following the Western campaign; after Rommel sent to him a specially prepared diary on the

7th Division, he received a letter of thanks from the dictator[429,430]</ref> (According to Speer, normally, he would send extremely unclear reports which annoyed Hitler greatly[431]). According to Maurice Remy, the relationship, which Remy calls "a dream marriage", only showed the first crack in 1942,[432] and later gradually turned into, in the words of German writer Ernst Jünger who was in contact with Rommel in Normandy, "hassliebe" (a love-hate relationship).[433] Ruge's diary and Rommel's letter to his wife showed his mood to fluctuate wildly regarding Hitler: while he showed disgust towards the atrocities and disappointment towards the situation, he was overjoyed to welcome a visit from Hitler, only to return to depression the next day when faced with reality.[434] Hitler displayed the same emotions. Amid growing doubts and differences, he would remain eager to hear from Rommel's calls (they had almost daily, hour-long, highly animated conversations, with the preferred topic being technical innovations[435]), once almost grabbed the telephone out of Linge's hand. Hitler tried to fix the dysfunctional relationship many times without results, with Rommel calling his attempts "Sunlamp Treatment", although later he said that "Once I have loved the Führer, and I still do."[6,436] Remy and *Der Spiegel* remark that the statement was very much genuine, while Watson notes that he believed he deserved to die for his treasonable plan.[437]

Rommel was an ambitious man who took advantage of his proximity to Hitler and willingly accepted the propaganda campaigns designed for him by Goebbels.[422,438]</ref> On one hand, he wanted personal promotion and the realization of his ideals. On the other hand, being elevated by the traditional system that gave preferential treatment to aristocratic officers would be betrayal of his aspiration "to remain a man of the troops".[439]</ref> In 1918, Rommel refused an invitation to a prestigious officer training course, and with it, the chance to be promoted to general.[440] Additionally, he had no inclination towards the political route, preferring to remain a soldier ("Nur-Soldat").[441] He was thus attracted by the Common Man theme which promised to level German society,[442] the glorification of the national community, and the idea of a soldier of common background who served the Fatherland with talent and got rewarded by another common man who embodied the will of the German people.[442] While he had much indignation towards German's contemporary class problem, this self-association with the Common Men went along well with his desire to simulate the knights of the past, who also led from the front.[443] (the dominant parent in Rommel's life was his mother Helene, a minor "von" and a loving, but ambitious and class-conscious mother who strongly stirred him towards a military career[9,444,445]) While Rommel was greatly attached to his profession ("the body and soul of war", a fellow officer commented),[446] he seemed to equally enjoy the idea of peace, as shown by his words to his wife in August 1939: "You can trust me, we have taken part in one World War, but as long as our generation live, there will not be a second.", as well as his letter sent to her the night before the Invasion of Poland, in which he expressed "boundless optimism" (Maurice Remy's comment): "I still believe the atmosphere will not become more bellicose."[447] Butler remarks that Rommel was center in his politics, leaning a little to the left in his attitude.[448]

Messenger argues that Rommel's attitude towards Hitler changed only after the Allied invasion of Normandy, when Rommel came to realise that the war could not be won,[424] while Maurice Remy suggests that Rommel never truly broke away from the relationship with Hitler, but praises him for "always had the courage to oppose him whenever his conscience required so."[432] The historian Peter Lieb states that it was not clear whether the threat of defeat was the only reason he wanted to switch sides The relationship seemed to go downhill much after a conversation in July 1943, in which Hitler told Rommel that if they did not win the war, the Germans could rot. Rommel even began to think that it was lucky that his Afrika Korps was now safe as POWs and could escape Hitler's Wagnerian ending.[449,450,451] Die Welt comments that Hitler chose Rommel as his favourite because he was apolitical, and that the combination of his military expertise and circumstances allowed Rommel to remain clean.

Rommel's political inclinations were a controversial matter even among the contemporary Nazi elites. Rommel himself, while showing support to some facets of the Nazi ideology and enjoying the propaganda the Nazi machine built around him, was enraged by the Nazi media's effort to portray him as an early party member and son of a mason, forcing them to correct these wrong facts.[452] The Nazi elites were not comfortable with the idea of a national icon who did not wholeheartedly support the regime. Hitler and Goebbels, his main supporters, tended to defend him. When Rommel was being considered for appointment as Commander-in-Chief of the Army in the summer of 1942, Goebbels wrote in his diary that Rommel "is ideologically sound, is not just sympathetic to the National Socialists. He is a National Socialist; he is a troop leader with a gift for improvisation, personally courageous and extraordinarily inventive. These are the kinds of soldiers we need."[423] Despite this, they gradually saw that his grasp of political realities and his views could be very different from theirs.[453]</ref> Hitler knew, though, that Rommel's optimistic and combative character was indispensable for his war efforts. When Rommel lost faith in the final victory and Hitler's leadership, Hitler and Goebbels tried to find an alternative in Manstein to remedy the fighting will and "political direction" of other generals but did not succeed.[454]

Meanwhile, officials who did not like Rommel like Bormann and Schirach whispered to each other that he was not a Nazi at all.[455] Rommel's relationship to the Nazi elites, other than Hitler and Goebbels, was mostly hostile, although even powerful people like Bormann[456] and Himmler had to tread carefully around Rommel. Himmler, who played a decisive role in Rommel's death, tried to blame Keitel and Jodl for the deed, which indeed was initiated by Keitel and Jodl, who deeply resented Rommel's meteoric rise and had long feared that he would become the Commander-in-Chief. (while Hitler also played innocent by trying to erect a monument for the national hero, on 7 March 1945) Franz Halder, after concocting several schemes to rein in Rommel through people like Paulus and Gause to no avail (even willing to undermine German operations and strategy in the process for the sole purpose of embarrassing him[305]), concluded that Rommel was a madman with whom no one dared to cross swords because of "his brutal methods and his backing from the highest levels".[457,458] Rommel for his part was highly critical of Himmler, Halder, the High Command and particularly Goering who Rommel at one point called his "bitterest enemy".[459]</ref> Hitler realized that Rommel attracted the elites' negative emotions to himself, in the same way he generated optimism in the common people. Depending on the case, Hitler manipulated or exarcebated the situation in order to benefit himself,[460,461]</ref> although he originally had no intent of pushing Rommel to the point of destruction (even after having been informed of Rommel's involvement in the plot, hurt and vengeful,[6] at first he wanted to retire Rommel,[462] and eventually offered him a last-minute chance to explain himself and refute the claims, which Rommel apparently did not take advantage of), until Rommel's enemies worked together to bring him down.

Maurice Remy concludes that, unwillingly and probably without ever realising, Rommel was part of a murderous regime, although he never actually grasped the core of National Socialism.[463] Peter Lieb sees Rommel as a person who could not be put into a single drawer, although problematic by modern moral standards, and suggests people to personally decide for themselves whether Rommel should remain a role model or not. Historian Cornelia Hecht remarks "It is really hard to know who the man behind the myth was," noting that in numerous letters he wrote to his wife during their almost 30-year marriage, he commented little on political issues as well as his personal life as a husband and a father.

Rommel myth

According to some critical authors, an assessment of Rommel's role in history has been hampered by views of Rommel that were formed, at least in part, due to political reasons, creating what these historians have called the "Rommel myth". The interpretation considered by some historians to be a myth is the depiction of the Field Marshal as an apolitical, brilliant commander and a victim of the Third Reich who participated in the 20 July plot against Adolf Hitler.[464,465] There is a notable number of authors who refer to "Rommel Myth" or "Rommel Legend" in a neutral or positive manner though.[466]</ref>[467]

The seeds of the myth can be found first in Rommel's drive for success as a young officer in World War I, and then in his popular 1937 book *Infantry Attacks*, which was written in a style that diverged from the German military literature of the time and became a bestseller.[468,87]

The myth then took shape during the opening years of World War II, as a component of Nazi propaganda to praise the Wehrmacht and instill optimism in the German public, with Rommel's willing participation. When Rommel came to North Africa, it was picked up and disseminated in the West by the British press as the Allies sought to explain their continued inability to defeat the Axis forces in North Africa.[469] The British military and political figures contributed to the heroic image of the man as Rommel resumed offensive operations in January 1942 against the British forces weakened by redeployments to the Far East. During parliamentary debate following the fall of Tobruk, Churchill described Rommel as an "extraordinary bold and clever opponent" and a "great field commander".[400,401]

According to *Der Spiegel*, following the war's end, West Germany yearned for father figures who were needed to replace the former ones who had been unmasked as criminals. Rommel was chosen because he embodied the decent soldier, cunning yet fair-minded, and if guilty by association, not so guilty that he became unreliable, and additionally, former comrades reported that he was close to the Resistance.[6] While everyone else was disgraced, his star became brighter than ever, and he made the historically unprecedent leap over the threshold between eras: from Hitler's favourite general, to the young republic's hero. Cornelia Hecht notes that despite the change of times, Rommel has become the symbol of different regimes and concepts, which is paradoxical, whoever the man he really was. Ulrich vom Hagen reports that Rommel, for the admiration shown towards him by all sides after the war, was used as a unity symbol that led to the "elegant settlement" of the conflict between fascistic, small-bourgeois elements and the aristocratic traditionalists during the early years after the formation of the Bundeswehr. Simon Ball describes how various elements in the German and British armies and governments extensively used Rommel's image in dealing with their inner struggles, promoting aspects of his that each group associated with themselves. Eric Dorman-Smith claimed that it was a "pity we could not have combined with Rommel to clean up the whole mess on both sides".[470]

At the same time, the Western Allies, and particularly the British, depicted Rommel as the "good German". His reputation for conducting a clean war was used in the interest of the West German rearmament and reconciliation between the former enemies—Britain and the United States on one side and the new Federal Republic of Germany on the other.[471] When Rommel's alleged involvement in the plot to kill Hitler became known after the war, his stature was enhanced in the eyes of his former adversaries. Rommel was often cited in Western sources as a patriotic German willing to stand up to Hitler. Churchill wrote about him in 1950: "[Rommel] (...) deserves our respect because, although a loyal German soldier, he came to hate Hitler and all his works, and took part in the conspiracy of 1944 to rescue Germany by displacing the maniac and tyrant."[472]

Foundational works

The German rearmament of the early 1950s was highly dependent on the moral rehabilitation that the Wehrmacht needed. The journalist and historian Basil Liddell Hart, an early proponent of these two interconnected initiatives, provided the first widely available source on Rommel in his 1948 book on Hitler's generals, updated in 1951, portraying Rommel in a positive light and as someone who stood apart from the regime.[473]

The other foundational text was the influential and laudatory 1950 biography *Rommel: The Desert Fox* by Brigadier Desmond Young.[474,475,476] Young extensively interviewed Rommel's widow and collaborated with several individuals who had been close to Rommel, including Hans Speidel. The manner of Rommel's death had led to the assumption that he had not been a supporter of Nazism, to which Young subscribed.[471,477,478]</ref> The reception of *The Desert Fox* in Britain was enthusiastic, with the book going through eight editions in a year.[479] Young's biography was another step in the development of the Rommel myth – with Rommel emerging as an active, if not a leading, plotter. Speidel contributed as well, starting, from the early 1950s, to bring up Rommel's and his own role in the plot, boosting his [Speidel's] suitability for a future role in the new military force of the Federal Republic, the Bundeswehr, and then in NATO.[480]

Further in 1953 was the publication of Rommel's writings of the war period as *The Rommel Papers*, edited by Liddell Hart.[481] The book contributed to the perception of Rommel as a brilliant commander; in an introduction, Liddell Hart drew comparisons between Rommel and Lawrence of Arabia, "two masters of desert warfare".[482] Liddell Hart had a personal interest in the work: by having coaxed Rommel's widow to include material favorable to himself, he could present Rommel as his "pupil". The controversy was described by the political scientist John Mearsheimer, who concluded that, by "manipulating history", Liddell Hart was in a position to show that he was at the root of the dramatic German success in 1940.[483,484]

Figure 34: *Rommel's desert uniform and death mask (right) displayed at the German Tank Museum in Munster.*

Elements of the myth

According to Connelly, Young and Liddell Hart laid the foundation for the Anglo-American myth, which consisted of three themes: Rommel's ambivalence towards Nazism; his military genius; and the emphasis of the chivalrous nature of the fighting in North Africa.[481] Their works lent support to the image of the "clean Wehrmacht" and were generally not questioned, since they came from British authors, rather than German revisionists.[485,486]</ref>

Historian Bruce Allen Watson offers his interpretation of the myth, encompassing the foundation laid down by the Nazi propaganda machine. According to Watson, the most dominant element is Rommel the Superior Soldier; the second being Rommel the Common Man; and the last one Rommel the Martyr.[487] The German news magazine *Der Spiegel* described the myth in 2007 as "Gentleman warrior, military genius".[488,489]</ref>

Contradictions and ambiguities

During recent years, historians' opinions on Rommel have become more diversified, with some aspects of his image being the target of revisionism more frequently than the others. According to the prominent German historian Hans-Ulrich Wehler, the modern consensus agrees with post-war sources that

Rommel treated the Allied captives decently, and he personally thinks that the movie *Rommel* does not overstate his conscience. Also according to Wehler, scholars in England and the US still show a lot of admiration towards Rommel the military commander. Some authors, notably Wolfgang Proske, see Rommel as a criminal whose memorials should be removed, although these represent the unorthodox minority (which is admitted by Proske). Perry and Massari note that the majority of historians continue to describe Rommel as a brilliant, chivalrous commander.[372]

Modern historians who agree with the image of the apolitical, chivalrous genius[490,491,492,493,494,495] also have different opinions regarding details. Smith and Bierman opine that Rommel might be considered an honourable man in his limited way but in a deeply dishonourable cause, and that he played the game of war with no more hatred for his opponent than a rugby team captain might feel for his opposite number. Butler states that Rommel's idealistic character led to grave misjudgements because he refused to let anything compromise it, and also that although he had a sense of strategy that developed greatly during the war, he lacked a philosophy of war.[496]

According to some modern scholars, he was much more complex than the figure that has been firmly established in post-war reputation.[497] Caddick-Adams writes that Rommel was a "complicated man of many contradictions",[498] while Beckett notes that "Rommel's myth (...) has proved remarkably resilient" and that more work is needed to put him in proper historical context.[252] Watson opines that historians often portray Rommel as someone they want him to be, "coward ... hero, fool, villain or hypocrite", and that he seemed to be all of these things, except coward, with perhaps a naive loyalty.[499] Hansen counters that Rommel was hardly naive, always judged military and political situations with cold objectivity, and shared a lot of characteristics with Hitler,[500] an opinion shared by psychoanalyst and historian Geoffrey Cocks, who writes that Rommel "embodies the modern synergy of technical expertise and self-promotion ... arriviste, ... professionally ambitious, adept at cultivating a mass media image ... like Hitler."

There is also, especially in Germany, an increasing tendency to portray Rommel as someone who cannot be explained in concrete details yet. However, these modern authors, while respecting the man and his mythical aura, are not afraid to show his questionable traits, or point out the horrible (including the possible) consequences of his "politically extremely naive" actions that perhaps would not be fitting of a role model, and allow living witnesses who might portray Rommel in a negative light to speak in documentaries about him, to the extent some, like General Storbeck, consider excessive and unbalanced

(Storbeck states that there are many other witnesses who will provide the opposite views, and also questions the use of an extremely ill Manfred Rommel to achieve a portrayal filmmakers want).[501]

Reputation as military commander

Rommel had been extraordinarily well known in his lifetime, including by his adversaries. His tactical prowess and consistent decency in the treatment of Allied prisoners earned him the respect of many opponents, including Claude Auchinleck, Archibald Wavell, George S. Patton, and Bernard Montgomery.[502]

Rommel's military reputation has been controversial. While nearly all military practitioners acknowledge Rommel's excellent tactical skills and personal bravery, some, such as U.S. major general and military historian David T. Zabecki of the United States Naval Institute, considers Rommel's performance as an operational level commander to be highly overrated. He argues that other officers share this belief.[63,503]</ref> General Klaus Naumann, who served as Chief of Staff of the Bundeswehr, agrees with the military historian Charles Messenger that Rommel had challenges at the operational level, and states that Rommel's violation of the unity of command principle, bypassing the chain of command in Africa, was unacceptable and contributed to the eventual operational and strategic failure in North Africa.[504,505]</ref> The German biographer Wolf Heckmann describes Rommel as "the most overrated commander of an army in world history".[506]

Nevertheless, there is also a notable number of officers who admire his methods, like Norman Schwarzkopf who describes Rommel as a "genius at battles of movement" and explains that "Look at Rommel. Look at North Africa, the Arab-Israeli wars, and all the rest of them. A war in the desert is a war of mobility and lethality. It's not a war where straight lines are drawn in the sand and [you] say, 'I will defend here or die." Ariel Sharon deemed the German military model used by Rommel to be superior to the British model used by Montgomery. His compatriot Moshe Dayan likewise considered Rommel a model and icon. Wesley Clark states that "Rommel's military reputation, though, has lived on, and still sets the standard for a style of daring, charismatic leadership to which most officers aspire." During the recent desert wars, Rommel's military theories and experiences attracted great interest from policy makers and military instructors. Chinese military leader Sun Li-jen had the laudatory nickname "Rommel of the East". The Bundeswehr and Germany's NATO partners recognize Rommel as the modern knight of the Bundeswehr, a highly successful operator of military arts and an apolitical, chivalrous soldier (with several leaders of the Bundeswehr like Helmut Willmann, Hartmut Bagger and Edgar Trost declaring him as their personal role model). This ideal of modern knighthood is connected and combined with the anachronistic Miles Christianus model, the more recent "Miles Protector" model,[507] the "Soldier-Statesman" concept, and the traditional monofunctional combatant.[508]

Certain modern military historians, such as Larry T. Addington, Niall Barr, Douglas Porch and Robert Citino, are skeptical of Rommel as an operational, let alone strategic level commander. They point to Rommel's lack of appreciation for Germany's strategic situation, his misunderstanding of the relative importance of his theatre to the German High Command, his poor grasp of logistical realities, and, according to the historian Ian Beckett, his "penchant for glory hunting".[497,396] Citino credits Rommel's limitations as an operational level commander as "materially contributing" to the eventual demise of the Axis forces in North Africa,[396,509] </ref> while Addington focuses on the struggle over strategy, whereby Rommel's initial brilliant success resulted in "catastrophic effects" for Germany in North Africa.[510] Porch highlights Rommel's "offensive mentality", symptomatic of the Wehrmacht commanders as a whole in the belief that the tactical and operational victories would lead to strategic success. Compounding the problem was the Wehrmacht's institutional tendency to discount logistics, industrial output and their opponents' capacity to learn from past mistakes.[511]

The historian Geoffrey P. Megargee points out Rommel's playing the German and Italian command structures against each other to his advantage. Rommel used the confused structure (the OKW (Supreme Command of the Wehrmacht), the OKH (Supreme High Command of the Army) and the Italian Supreme Command) to disregard orders that he disagreed with or to appeal to whatever authority he felt would be most sympathetic to his requests.[512]

Some historians, such as Zabecki and Peter Lieb, take issue with Rommel's absence from Normandy on the day of the Allied invasion, 6 June 1944. He had left France on 5 June and was at home on the 6th celebrating his wife's birthday. (According to Rommel, he planned to proceed to see Hitler the next day to discuss the situation in Normandy).[513,514] Zabecki calls his decision to leave the theatre in view of an imminent invasion "an incredible lapse of command responsibility".[513]

T.L.McMahon argues that Rommel no doubt possessed operational vision, however Rommel did not have the strategic resources to effect his operational choices while his forces provided the tactical ability to accomplish his goals, and the German staff and system of staff command were designed for commanders who led from the front, and in some cases he might have chosen the same options as Montgomery (a reputedly strategy-oriented commander) had he been put in the same conditions. According to Steven Zaloga, tactical flexibility was a great advantage of the German system, but in the final years of the war, Hitler and his cronies like Himmler and Goering had usurped more and more authority at the strategic level, leaving professionals like Rommel increasing constraints on their actions. Martin Blumenson considers Rommel a general with a compelling view of strategy and logistics, which was demonstrated through his many arguments with his superiors over such matters, although Blumenson also thinks that what distinguished Rommel was his boldness, his intuitive feel for the battlefield.(Upon which Schwarzkopf also comments "Rommel had a feel for the battlefield like no other man.")

Joseph Forbes comments that: "The complex, conflict-filled interaction between Rommel and his superiors over logistics, objectives and priorities should not be used to detract from Rommel's reputation as a remarkable military leader", because Rommel was not given powers over logistics, and because if only generals who attain strategic-policy goals are great generals, such highly regarded commanders as Robert E. Lee, Hannibal, Charles XII would have to be excluded from that list. General Siegfried F. Storbeck, Deputy Inspector General of the Bundeswehr (1987–1991), remarks that, Rommel's leadership style and offensive thinking, although carrying inherent risks like losing the overview of the situation and creating overlapping of authority, have been proved effective, and have been analysed and incorporated in the training of officers by "us, our Western allies, the Warsaw Pact, and even the Israel Defense Forces." Maurice Remy and Samuel Mitcham both defend his strategic decision regarding Malta as, although risky, the only logical choice.[515]</ref>[516]</ref> Mitcham also takes note of the fact that the British C-in-C actually feared that the German leadership would embark on Rommel's strategic plans regarding the Suez Canal instead of that of Hitler.[517]

Rommel was among the few Axis commanders (the others being Isoroku Yamamoto and Reinhard Heydrich) who were targeted for assassination by Allied planners. Two attempts were made, the first being Operation Flipper in North Africa in 1941, and the second being Operation Gaff in Normandy in 1944.[518]

Family life

While at Cadet School in 1911, Rommel met and became engaged to 17-year-old Lucia (Lucie) Maria Mollin (1894–1971).[20] While stationed in Weingarten in 1913, Rommel developed a relationship with Walburga Stemmer, which produced a daughter, Gertrude, born 8 December 1913.[519] Because of elitism in the officer corps, Stemmer's working-class background made her unsuitable as an officer's wife, and Rommel felt honour-bound to uphold his previous

Figure 35: *Bust of Rommel at Al Alamein war museum in Egypt, which was built by Anwar Sadat in honour of Rommel. The museum was later expanded into a general war museum but Rommel remains a central figure.*[524]

commitment to Mollin. With Mollin's cooperation, he accepted financial responsibility for the child.[520] Rommel and Mollin were married in November 1916 in Danzig.[20] Rommel's marriage was a happy one, and he wrote his wife at least one letter every day while he was in the field.[20]

After the end of the First World War, the couple settled initially in Stuttgart, and Stemmer and her child lived with them. Gertrude was referred to as Rommel's niece, a fiction that went unquestioned due to the enormous number of women widowed during the war.[521] Walburga died suddenly in October 1928, and Gertrude remained a member of the household until Rommel's death in 1944.[522] A son, Manfred Rommel, was born on 24 December 1928, later served as Mayor of Stuttgart from 1974 to 1996.[523]

Awards

- Military Merit Order (Württemberg)[525]
- Iron Cross 2nd Class on 24 September 1914 & 1st Class on 29 January 1915[526]
- Pour le Mérite on 18 December 1917[527]

- Clasp to the Iron Cross 2nd Class on 13 May 1940 & 1st Class on 15 May 1940[528]
- Knight's Cross of the Iron Cross with Oak Leaves, Swords and Diamonds
  - Knight's Cross of the Iron Cross on 27 May 1940 as commander of the 7th Panzer-Division[529]
  - Oak Leaves (10th recipient) on 20 March 1941 as commander of the 7th Panzer-Division[529]
  - Swords (6th recipient) on 20 January 1942 as commander of the Panzer Group Afrika[529]
  - Diamonds (6th recipient) on 11 March 1943 as commander in chief of the Army Group Afrika[529]
- Italian Gold Medal of Military Valour in February 1942[530]
- Knight of the Colonial Order of the Star of Italy in February 1942[530]

Posthumous honours

The German Army's largest base, the Field Marshal Rommel Barracks, Augustdorf, is named in his honour; at the dedication in 1961 his widow Lucie and son Manfred Rommel were guests of honour.[531] The Rommel Barracks, Dornstadt, was also named for him in 1965. A third base named for him, the Field Marshal Rommel Barracks, Osterode, closed in 2004. A German Navy Lütjens-class destroyer, *Rommel*, was named for him in 1969 and christened by his widow; the ship was decommissioned in 1998.[532]

Numerous streets in Germany, especially in Rommel's home state of Baden-Württemberg, are named in his honor, including the street near where his last home was located. The Rommel Memorial was erected in Heidenheim in 1961. The Rommel Museum opened in 1989 in the Villa Lindenhof in Herrlingen;[533] there is also a Rommel Museum in Mersa Matruh in Egypt which opened in 1977, and which is located in one of Rommel's former headquarters; various other localities and establishments in Mersa Matruh, including Rommel Beach, are also named for Rommel.[534]

In Italy, the annual marathon tour "Rommel Trail", which is sponsored by the Protezione Civile and the autonomous region of Friuli Venezia Giulia through its tourism agency, celebrates Rommel and the Battle of Caporetto. The naming has been criticized by the politician Giuseppe Civati.

References

Informational notes

Citations

Bibliography <templatestyles src="Template:Refbegin/styles.css" />

- Addington, Larry H. (1967). "Operation Sunflower: Rommel Versus the General Staff"[535]. *Military Affairs*. **31** (3): 120.
- Atkinson, Rick (2013). *The Guns at Last Light* (1 ed.). New York: Henry Holt and Company. ISBN 978-0-8050-6290-8.
- Barr, Niall (2014). "Rommel in the Desert, 1941". In I.F.W. Beckett. *Rommel Reconsidered*. Mechanicsburg, PA: Stackpole Books. ISBN 978-0-8117-1462-4.
- Beckett, Ian F.W., ed. (2014). *Rommel Reconsidered*. Stackpole Books. ISBN 978-0-8117-1462-4.
- Ball, Simon (17 August 2016). *Alamein: Great Battles*[536]. Oxford University Press,. ISBN 978-0-19-150462-4.
- Beevor, Antony (2009). *D-Day: The Battle for Normandy*. New York: Viking. ISBN 978-0-670-02119-2.
- Benishay, Guitel (4 May 2016). "Le journal de bord du chef SS en Tunisie découvert"[537]. Création Bereshit Agency. LPH info - Création Bereshit Agency. Retrieved 18 July 2017.
- Blumentritt, Günther (1952). *Von Rundstedt: The Soldier and the Man*[538]. Odhams Press.
- Brighton, Terry (2008). *Patton, Montgomery, Rommel: Masters of War*. New York: Crown. ISBN 978-0-307-46154-4.
- Bradford, Ernie (2011). *Siege Malta 1940–1943*[539]. Pen and Sword. pp. 66, 183. ISBN 978-1-84884-584-8.
- Butler, Daniel Allen (2015). *Field Marshal: The Life and Death of Erwin Rommel*[540]. Havertown, PA / Oxford: Casemate. ISBN 978-1-61200-297-2.
- Butler, Rupert (3 March 2016). *SS Hitlerjugend: The History of the Twelfth SS Division, 1943–45*[541]. Amber Books Ltd,. ISBN 978-1-78274-294-4.
- Caddick-Adams, Peter (2012). *Monty and Rommel: Parallel Lives*. New York, NY: The Overlook Press. ISBN 978-1-59020-725-3.
- Carver, Michael (1962). *El Alamein*. Ware, Hertfordshire: Wordsworth Editions. ISBN 978-1-84022-220-3.
- Carver, Michael (2005). *The Warlords*[542]. Pen and Sword. ISBN 9781473819740.
- Churchill, Winston (1949). *Their Finest Hour*. The Second World War. **II**. Boston; Toronto: Houghton Mifflin. OCLC 396145[543].
- —— (1950). *The Grand Alliance*. The Second World War. **III**. Boston; Toronto: Houghton Mifflin. OCLC 396147[544].
- Citino, Robert (2012). "Rommel's Afrika Korps"[545]. *HistoryNet*. Retrieved 3 March 2016.
- Coggins, Jack (1980). *The Campaign for North Africa*. New York: Doubleday & Company. ISBN 0-385-04351-1.

- Cohen, Nir (17 April 2015). "Inside the diary of SS officer known as gas chamber 'mastermind'"[546]. Yedioth Internet. Ynetnews. Retrieved 18 July 2017.
- Connelly, Mark (2014). "Rommel as icon". In F.W. Beckett (editor). *Rommel Reconsidered*. Mechanicsburg, PA: Stackpole Books. ISBN 978-0-8117-1462-4.
- Douglas-Home, Charles (1973). *Rommel. The Great Commanders*. New York: Saturday Review Press. ISBN 0-8415-0255-2.
- Evans, Richard J. (2009). *The Third Reich at War*. New York: Penguin. ISBN 978-0-14-101548-4.
- Faltin, Thomas (2014). "Haus der Geschichte in Stuttgart - Erwin Rommel kannte wohl Pläne für Hitler-Attentat"[547]. Stuttgarter Zeitung. Retrieved 7 August 2016.
- Finklestone, Joseph (2013). *Anwar Sadat: Visionary Who Dared*[548]. Routledge. p. 16. ISBN 1135195587. Retrieved 8 October 2017.
- Von Fleischhauer, Jan; Friedmann, Jan (2012). "Die Kraft des Bösen"[549]. *Der Spiegel* (in German) (44). Retrieved 3 August 2016.
- Forty, George (1997). *The Armies of Rommel*. Arms and Armour. p. 342. ISBN 978-1-85409-379-0.
- Fraser, David (1993). *Knight's Cross: A Life of Field Marshal Erwin Rommel*. New York: HarperCollins. ISBN 978-0-06-018222-9.
- Friedmann, Jan (23 May 2007). "World War II: New Research Taints Image of Desert Fox Rommel"[550]. *Spiegel Online*. Retrieved 4 March 2016.
- Green, Leslie C. (1993). *The Contemporary Law of Armed Conflict*. Manchester University Press. ISBN 978-0-7190-3540-1.
- Hart, Russel A. (2014). "Rommel and the 20th July Bomb Plot". In Ian F.W. Beckett. *Rommel Reconsidered*. Stackpole Books. ISBN 978-0-8117-1462-4.
- Hoffmann, Karl (2004). *Erwin Rommel, 1891–1944*. Commanders in Focus. London: Brassey's. ISBN 1-85753-374-7.
- Holderfield, Randy; Varhola, Michael (2009). *D-day: The Invasion of Normandy, June 6, 1944*. Da Capo Press. ISBN 978-0-7867-4680-4.
- Holmes, Richard (2009). *World War II: The Definitive Visual History*[551]. Penguin. p. 129. ISBN 978-0-7566-5605-8.
- House, J. M. (1985). *Toward Combined Arms Warfare: A Survey of 20th-century Tactics, Doctrine, and Organization*[552]. DIANE Publishing. ISBN 9781428915831.
- Kitchen, Martin (2009). *Rommel's Desert War: Waging World War II in North Africa, 1941–1943*. Cambridge University Press. ISBN 978-0-521-50971-8.
- Krause, Michael D.; Phillips, R. Cody (2007). *Historical Perspectives of*

- *the Operational Art.* Center of Military History - US Army. ISBN 978-0-16-072564-7.
- Latimer, Jon (2002). *Alamein.* Cambridge, MA: Harvard University Press. ISBN 978-0-674-01016-1.
- Lewin, Ronald (1998) [1968]. *Rommel As Military Commander.* New York: B&N Books. ISBN 978-0-7607-0861-3.
- Lieb, Peter (2013). "Ardenne Abbey Massacre". In Mikaberidze, Alexander. *Atrocities, Massacres, and War Crimes: An Encyclopedia.* Santa Barbara, Calif: ABC-CLIO. pp. 25–27. ISBN 1-59884-926-3.
- —— (2014). "Rommel in Normandy". In I.F.W. Beckett. *Rommel Reconsidered.* Mechanicsburg, PA: Stackpole Books. ISBN 978-0-8117-1462-4.
- von Luck, Hans (1989). *Panzer Commander: The Memoirs of Colonel Hans von Luck.* New York: Dell Publishing of Random House. ISBN 0-440-20802-5.
- Luvaas, Jay (1990). "Liddell Hart and the Mearsheimer Critique: A "Pupil's" Retrospective"[553] (PDF). *Strategic Studies Institute.* Retrieved 8 February 2016.
- Maier, Manfred (2013). "Vortrag Manfred Maier zu der Geschichte des Heidenheimer Rommeldenkmals". In Geschichtswerkstatt Heidenheim. *Vorlage für die Arbeitsgruppe «Umgestaltung des Rommel-Denkmals».* p. 49.
- Major, Patrick (2008). "'Our Friend Rommel': The Wehrmacht as 'Worthy Enemy' in Postwar British Popular Culture". *German History.* Oxford University Press. **26** (4): 520–535. doi: 10.1093/gerhis/ghn049[554].
- Mearsheimer, John (1988). *Liddell Hart and the Weight of History.* Ithaca, N.Y.: Cornell University Press. ISBN 978-0-8014-2089-4.
- Megargee, Geoffrey P. (2000). *Inside Hitler's High Command.* Lawrence, Kansas: Kansas University Press. ISBN 0-7006-1015-4.
- von Mellenthin, Friedrich (1956). *Panzer Battles: A Study of the Employment of Armor in the Second World War.* London: Cassell. ISBN 978-0-345-32158-9.
- Messenger, Charles (2009). *Rommel: Leadership Lessons from the Desert Fox.* Basingstoke, NY: Palgrave Macmillan. ISBN 0-230-60908-2.
- Mitcham, Samuel (1997). *The Desert Fox in Normandy: Rommel's Defense of Fortress Europe*[555]. p. 198. ISBN 0-275-95484-6.
- Mitcham, Samuel W. (2007). *Rommel's Desert Commanders — The Men Who Served the Desert Fox, North Africa, 1941–42.* Mechanicsburg, PA: Stackpole Books. ISBN 0-8117-3510-9.
- —— (2008). *The Rise of the Wehrmacht.* Westport, Conn.: Praeger Security International. ISBN 978-0-275-99641-3.

- Moorhouse, Roger (2007). *Killing Hitler: The Third Reich and the Plots Against the Führer*. London: Random House. ISBN 978-1-84413-322-2.
- Murray, Williamson; Millett, Allan Reed (2009). *A War To Be Won: fighting the Second World War*. Harvard University Press. ISBN 978-0-674-04130-1.
- Naumann, Klaus (2009). "Afterword". In Charles Messenger. *Rommel: Leadership Lessons from the Desert Fox*. Basingstoke, NY: Palgrave Macmillan. ISBN 0-230-60908-2.
- Perry, Marvin (22 February 2012). *World War II in Europe: A Concise History*[556]. Cengage Learning. p. 165. ISBN 1-285-40179-4.
- Pimlott, John, ed. (1994). *Rommel: In His Own Words*. London: Greenhill Books. ISBN 978-1-85367-185-2.
- —— (2003). *Rommel and His Art of War*. Greenhill Books. ISBN 978-1-85367-543-0.
- Playfair, Major-General I. S. O.; with Flynn, Captain F. C. RN; Molony, Brigadier C. J. C. & Gleave, Group Captain T. P. (2004) [1960 HMSO]. Butler, Sir James, ed. *The Mediterranean and Middle East: British Fortunes reach their Lowest Ebb (September 1941 to September 1942)*. History of the Second World War, United Kingdom Military Series. **III**. Uckfield, UK: Naval & Military Press. ISBN 1-84574-067-X.
- Porch, Douglas (2004). *The Path to Victory: The Mediterranean Theater in World War II* (1st ed.). New York: Farrar, Straus and Giroux. ISBN 978-0-374-20518-8.
- Remy, Maurice Philip (2002). *Mythos Rommel*[557] (in German). Munich: List Verlag. ISBN 3-471-78572-8.
- Reuth, Ralf Georg (2005). *Rommel: The End of a Legend*. London: Haus Books. ISBN 978-1-904950-20-2.
- Rice, Earle (2009). *Erwin J. E. Rommel-Great Military Leaders of the 20th Century Series*. Infobase.
- Rommel, Erwin (1982) [1953]. Liddell Hart, B. H., ed. *The Rommel Papers*[558]. New York: Da Capo Press. ISBN 978-0-306-80157-0.
- Sadler, John (2016). *El Alamein 1942: The Story of the Battle in the Words of the Soldiers*[559]. Bloomsbury Publishing. ISBN 978-1-4728-1490-6.
- Scheck, Raffael (2010). "Mythos Rommel (Raffael Scheck)"[560].
- Scherzer, Veit (2007). *Die Ritterkreuzträger 1939–1945 Die Inhaber des Ritterkreuzes des Eisernen Kreuzes 1939 von Heer, Luftwaffe, Kriegsmarine, Waffen-SS, Volkssturm sowie mit Deutschland verbündeter Streitkräfte nach den Unterlagen des Bundesarchives* [*The Knight's Cross Bearers 1939–1945 The Holders of the Knight's Cross of the Iron Cross 1939 by Army, Air Force, Navy, Waffen-SS, Volkssturm and Allied Forces with Germany According to the Documents of the Federal Archives*]

(in German). Jena, Germany: Scherzers Militaer-Verlag. ISBN 978-3-938845-17-2.
- Scianna, Bastian Matteo (2018). "Rommel Almighty? Italian Assessments of the 'Desert Fox' During and After the Second World War". *The Journal of Military History, Vol.82, Issue 1.* p. 125-145.
- Searle, Alaric (2014). "Rommel and the rise of the Nazis". In Beckett, Ian F.W. *Rommel Reconsidered*. Stackpole Books. ISBN 978-0-8117-1462-4.
- Shirer, William L. (1960). *The Rise and Fall of the Third Reich*. New York: Simon and Schuster. ISBN 978-0-671-62420-0.
- Showalter, Dennis (3 January 2006). *Patton And Rommel: Men of War in the Twentieth Century*[561]. Penguin. ISBN 978-1-4406-8468-5.
- Speidel, Hans (1950). *Invasion 1944: Rommel and the Normandy Campaign*. Chicago: Henry Regnery.
- Strawson, Major General John (2013). *If By Chance: Military Turning Points that Changed History*[562]. Pan Macmillan. p. 124. ISBN 978-1-4472-3553-8.
- Watson, Bruce Allen (1999). *Exit Rommel: The Tunisian Campaign, 1942–43*[563]. Westport, Conn.: Praeger Publishers. ISBN 978-0-275-95923-4.
- Willmott, H.P. (1984). *June, 1944*. Poole: Blandford Press. ISBN 0-7137-1446-8.
- Young, Desmond (1950). *Rommel: The Desert Fox*[564]. New York: Harper & Row. OCLC 48067797[565].
- Zabecki, David T. (2016). "Rethinking Rommel"[566]. *Military History*. Herndon, Va. **32** (5): 24–29.
- —— (2016). "March 2016 Readers' Letters"[567]. *HistoryNet*. Retrieved 3 March 2016.

Further reading <templatestyles src="Template:Refbegin/styles.css" />

- Bierman, John; Smith, Colin (2002). *The Battle of Alamein: Turning Point, World War II*. ISBN 978-0-670-03040-8.
- Chambers, Madeline (2012). "The Devil's General? German film seeks to debunk Rommel myth"[568]. *Reuters*. Retrieved 8 February 2016.
- Citino, Robert (2007). *Death of the Wehrmacht: The German Campaigns of 1942*[569]. University Press of Kansas.
- De Lannoy, Francois (2002). *Afrikakorps, 1941–1943: the Libya Egypt Campaign*. Bayeux: Heimdal. ISBN 978-2-84048-152-2.
- Gibson, Charles M. (2001). "Operational Leadership as Practiced by Field Marshall Erwin Rommel During the German Campaign in North Africa 1941–1942: Success of Failure?"[570] (PDF). *Naval War College*. Retrieved 15 February 2016.

- Greene, Jack; Massignani, Alessandro (1994). *Rommel's North Africa Campaign: September 1940 – November 1942*. Conshohocken, PA: Combined Books. ISBN 978-1-58097-018-1.
- Kelly, Orr (2002). *Meeting the Fox: The Allied Invasion of Africa, from Operation Torch to Kasserine Pass to Victory in Tunisia*. New York: J. Wiley. ISBN 978-0-471-41429-2.
- Kriebel, Rainer; Gudmundsson, Bruce I (1999). *Inside the Afrika Korps: The Crusader Battles, 1941–1942*. London: Greenhill. ISBN 978-1-85367-322-1.
- Latimer, Jon (2001). *Tobruk 1941: Rommel's Opening Move*. Oxford: Osprey Military. ISBN 978-1-84176-092-6.
- Marshall, Charles F. (1994). *The Rommel Murder: The Life and Death of the Desert Fox*. Stackpole Marshall Books. ISBN 978-0-8117-2472-2.
- Pyta, Wolfram (14 April 2015). *Hitler: Der Künstler als Politiker und Feldherr. Eine Herrschaftsanalyse*[571]. Siedler Verlag,. ISBN 978-3-641-15701-2.
- Robinson, James R. (1997). "The Rommel Myth"[572]. *Military Review Journal*. Retrieved 8 February 2016.
- Samuels, Martin (2017) "Erwin Rommel and German Military Doctrine, 1912-1940" *War in History* v.24 n.3 pp.308-35
- Scianna, Bastian Matteo (2018). "Rommel Almighty? Italian Assessments of the 'Desert Fox' During and After the Second World War". *The Journal of Military History, Vol.82, Issue 1*. p. 125-145.
- Thompson, Julian (2011) [2008]. *Dunkirk: Retreat to Victory*. New York: Arcade. ISBN 978-1-61145-314-0.
- Windrow, Martin (1976). *Rommel's Desert Army*. Osprey. ISBN 978-0-85045-095-8.

External links

- Works by or about Erwin Rommel[573] at Internet Archive
- Erwin Rommel[574]. Biography.com
- Neitzel, Sönke (2005), "Rommel, Eugen Johannes Erwin"[575], *Neue Deutsche Biographie (NDB)* (in German), **22**, Berlin: Duncker & Humblot, pp. 23–24; (full text online[576])
- Works by or about Erwin Rommel[577] in libraries (WorldCat catalog)
- "Defeating the Desert Fox": Video[578] on YouTube, via the official channel of The National WWII Museum; session by Nigel Hamilton at the 2012 International Conference on World War II
- "Erwin Rommel 1891–1944"[579]. *LeMO at Deutsches Historisches Museum* (in German). Retrieved 13 May 2016.

- Newspaper clippings about Erwin Rommel[580] in the 20th Century Press Archives of the German National Library of Economics (ZBW)

Rommel myth

Rommel myth

<indicator name="good-star"> ⊕ </indicator>

The **Rommel myth**, or the **Rommel legend**, is a phrase used by a number of historians in reference to common depictions of German field marshal Erwin Rommel as an apolitical, brilliant commander and a victim of Nazi Germany due to his participation in the 20 July plot against Adolf Hitler. According to these historians, who take a critical view of Rommel, such depictions are not accurate.

The myth was created, with Rommel's participation, as a component of Nazi propaganda to praise the Wehrmacht and instill optimism in the German public. Starting in 1941, it was picked up and disseminated in the West by the British war-time press as the Allies sought to explain their continued inability to defeat the Axis forces in North Africa.

Following the war, the Western Allies, and particularly the British, depicted Rommel as the "good German" and "our friend Rommel", adhering closely to the tenets of the myth of the clean Wehrmacht. His reputation for conducting a clean war was used in the interests of West German rearmament during the Cold War and the reconciliation between the former enemies—the United Kingdom and the United States on one side, and the new Federal Republic of Germany on the other. The 1950 biography *Rommel: The Desert Fox* and the 1953 publication of *The Rommel Papers* added to the myth, which has proven resilient to critical examination.

The mythology surrounding Rommel has been the subject of analysis by both English- and German-speaking historians in recent decades. The reevaluation has produced new interpretations of Rommel, including his relationship with National Socialism, his abilities as operational and strategic level commander, and his role (if any) in the July 20th plot to assassinate Hitler. Historians and commentators conclude that Rommel remains an ambiguous figure, not easily definable either inside or outside the myth.

Terminology

Early authors such as Desmond Young and Basil Liddell Hart mention "the Rommel legend" in their respective books. Liddell Hart described British efforts to make counterpropaganda against Rommel's military reputation (while showing respect to his conduct of war): "Thus the British commanders and headquarter staffs were compelled to make strenuous efforts to dispel 'the Rommel legend' ".[581,582] As early as 1950, Bernard Montgomery's former deputy referred to the "myth" in an article titled "The Rommel Myth Debunked" where he aimed to address perceived misconceptions regarding the fighting in the North African Campaign.[583]

As used by German authors, *Mythos Rommel* (roughly translated into English as "Rommel myth") is a neutral description, as can be seen in works by historians such as Peter Lieb.[584] The term recognizes, per Lieb, that "Rommel is and remains a *Mythos*... He could not be stuck in a single drawer. At any rate, one should decide for oneself whether one sees him as a role model or not". German authors who use the word "Mythos" in this neutral manner include Maurice Philip Remy, Wolfram Pyta,[585] Jörg Echternkamp,[586] Guido Knopp,[587] and Sandra Mass.[588]

Origins

The origins of the myth can be found first in Rommel's drive for success as a young officer in World War I, and then in his popular 1937 book *Infanterie Greift An (Infantry Attacks)* that was written in a style that diverged from the German military literature of the time. The book became a bestseller, and was supposedly read by Adolf Hitler.[589,590]

Historian Antony Beevor places the start of the "Rommel legend" on 13 May 1940, during the Battle of France, when Rommel's troops crossed the Meuse under fire and established bridgeheads at Houx and Dinant.[591]

Figure 36: *Rommel at the Paris victory parade, June 1940. Rommel had access to Reich Propaganda Minister Joseph Goebbels via Karl Hanke, who served under Rommel in 1940.*[592]

In Nazi and Allied propaganda

Rommel's victories in France were featured in the German press and in the February 1941 film *Sieg im Westen (Victory in the West)*, in which he personally helped direct a segment reenacting the crossing of the Somme River.[593] Rommel's victories in 1941 were played up by Nazi propaganda, even though his successes in North Africa were achieved in Germany's least strategically important theatre of World War II.[590,594] Martin Kitchen: "German historians have largely ignored the North African campaign, not only because it was peripheral ..."[595] James Robinson: "German thinking was disinterested with an expanded strategic purpose in North Africa and Rommel knew it."[596]</ref> In November 1941, Joseph Goebbels (head of the Reich Ministry of Propaganda) wrote about his intention to have Rommel "elevated to a kind of popular hero". Rommel, with his innate abilities as a military commander and love of the spotlight, was a perfect fit for the role Goebbels designed for him.[590]

In North Africa, Rommel received help in cultivating his image from Alfred Ingemar Berndt, a senior official at the Reich Propaganda Ministry, who had volunteered for military service.[597] Seconded by Goebbels, Berndt was assigned to Rommel's staff and became one of his closest aides. Berndt often acted as liaison between Rommel, the Propaganda Ministry and the Führer Headquarters. He directed Rommel's photo shoots and filed radio dispatches describing the battles.[598,599]

In the spring of 1941, Rommel's name began to appear in the British media. In the autumn of 1941 and early winter of 1941/1942, he was mentioned in the British press almost daily. The *Daily Express* and *The Cairns Post* wrote: "No 'von' nonsense about Erich, nor the code of conduct—such as it was—that most Prussian officers have honoured in war. He is a gangster general, trained in a harder school than Chicago. He was Hitler's thug organiser before he came to power ... So Erich became leader of the S.S. Black Guard, Hitler's private army, which executes his private revenges and guards his person ... When at last Poland made a stand for democracy, it was Rommel who led a panzer corps against the Polish horse cavalry with conspicuous gallantry. Later in France Hitler made him a Knight of the Iron Cross for breaking through the Maginot Line at Maubeuge with the 7th Armoured Division. True, French resistance was almost at an end then, but Erich was entitled to his decoration, too."[600,601] Toward the end of the year, the Reich propaganda machine also used Rommel's successes in Africa as a diversion from the Wehrmacht's challenging situation in the Soviet Union with the stall of Operation Barbarossa.[602,603,604]</ref> The American press soon began to take notice of Rommel as well, following the United States' entry into the war on 11 December 1941, writing that: "The British ... admire him because he beat them and were surprised to have beaten in turn such a capable general". General Claude Auchinleck distributed a directive to his commanders seeking to dispel the notion that Rommel was a "superman".[605,606] The Tunisian tug-of-war and the Battle of Kasserine Pass intensified the GIs' admiration towards Rommel. The cult of personality was so strong that, according to Peter Schrijvers, "for the remainder of the war, German POWs would part with pictures of Rommel as reluctantly as GIs were eager to get them".[607] While Allied troops respected Rommel, civilians held the "widely accepted" negative image of Rommel's origin and his connection with the Nazis.[608] As described by Rosie Goldschmidt Waldeck (who debunked the invented story) and *The New York Times in 1943*, "It has been said that Rommel started his career as a Hitler hoodlum and owes his quick rise to his early collaboration with Himmler."[608,609] This line of propaganda perpetuated until the war ended.[610]

The attention of the Western and especially the British press thrilled Goebbels, who wrote in his diary in early 1942: "Rommel continues to be the recognised darling of even the enemies' news agencies".[611] Rommel was pleased by the media attention, both domestic and foreign, often discussing it in letters to his wife.[611,612]</ref> Hitler took note of the British propaganda as well, commenting in the summer of 1942 that Britain's leaders must have hoped "to be able to explain their defeat to their own nation more easily by focusing on Rommel".[613]

Rommel was the German commander most frequently covered in the German media, and the only one to be given a press conference, which took place in October 1942.[599,614] The press conference was moderated by Goebbels and was attended by both domestic and foreign media. Rommel declared: "Today we ... have the gates of Egypt in hand, and with the intent to act!" Keeping the focus on Rommel distracted the German public from Wehrmacht losses elsewhere as the tide of the war began to turn. He became a symbol that was used to reinforce the German public's faith in an ultimate Axis victory.[615]

Military reverses

In the wake of the British victory at Second Battle of El Alamein in November 1942, and other military reverses, the Propaganda Ministry directed the media to emphasise Rommel's invincibility. The charade was maintained until the spring of 1943, even as the German situation in Africa became increasingly precarious. In May 1943, to ensure that the inevitable defeat in Africa would not be associated with Rommel's name, Goebbels had the Supreme High Command announce that Rommel was on a two-month leave for health reasons.[616,617]</ref> Instead, the campaign was presented by Berndt, who resumed his role in the Propaganda Ministry, as a ruse to tie down the British Empire while Germany was turning Europe into an impenetrable fortress, with Rommel at the helm of this success. After the radio program ran in May 1943, Rommel sent Berndt a case of cigars as a sign of his gratitude.[616]

Although Rommel then entered a period without a significant command,[618] he remained a household name in Germany, synonymous with the aura of invincibility.[619] Hitler then made Rommel part of his defensive strategy for "Fortress Europe" (*Festung Europa*) by sending him to the West to inspect fortifications along the Atlantic Wall. Goebbels supported the decision, noting in his diary that Rommel was "undoubtedly the suitable man" for the task. The propaganda minister expected the move to reassure the German public, and at the same time to have a negative impact on the Allied forces' morale.[619]

In France, a Wehrmacht propaganda company frequently accompanied Rommel on his inspection trips to document his work for both domestic and foreign audiences.[620,621] In May 1944, the German newsreels reported on Rommel's speech at a Wehrmacht conference, where he stated his conviction that "every single German soldier will make his contribution against the Anglo-American spirit that it deserves for its criminal and bestial air war campaign against our homeland." The speech led to an upswing in morale and sustained confidence in Rommel.[622]

Figure 37: *One of the many Nazi propaganda photographs of Rommel's inspection tours along the Atlantic Wall.*

When Rommel was seriously wounded on 17 July 1944, the Propaganda Ministry undertook efforts to conceal the injury so as not to undermine domestic morale. Despite this, the news leaked to the British press. To counteract the rumors of a serious injury and even death, Rommel was required to appear at a press conference held on 1 August. On 3 August, the German press published an official report that Rommel had been injured in a car accident. Rommel noted in his diary his dismay at this twisting of the truth, belatedly realising how much the Reich propaganda was using him for its own ends.[622]

Post-war

Quoting Correlli Barnett ("The Desert War entered the British folk-memory, a source of legend, endlessly re-written as both history and fiction"), the historian Lucio Ceva argues that even though the myth was of British origin, it found its reflections in post-war West Germany.[623] The historian Peter Caddick-Adams suggests that, following the forced suicide, Rommel emerged as the "acceptable face of German militarism, the 'good' German who stood apart from the Nazi regime."[624] The ground was thus fertile for the myth to be reborn after the war, in the interest of the program of the German rearmament and the Allied–West German reconciliation.[603,625]

After the outbreak of the Korean War in 1950, it became clear to the Americans and the British that a German army would have to be revived to help face off against the Soviet Union. Many former German officers, including Adolf Heusinger and Hans Speidel, who had served on Rommel's staff in France, were convinced that no future West German Army would be possible without the rehabilitation of the Wehrmacht. In October 1950, at the behest of West German chancellor Konrad Adenauer, a group of former senior officers produced the document that later became known as the Himmerod memorandum. Intended as both a planning and a negotiating tool, the document included a key demand for "measures to transform domestic and foreign public opinion" with regards to the German military.[626,627]

Foundational works

Rommel's former enemies, especially the British, played a key role in the manufacture and propagation of the myth.[590,628] The German rearmament was highly dependent on the moral rehabilitation that the Wehrmacht needed. The journalist and historian Basil Liddell Hart, an early proponent of these two interconnected initiatives, provided the first widely available source on Rommel in his 1948 book on Hitler's generals, updated in 1951. Portraying Rommel as an outsider to the Nazi regime in the 1948 edition, Liddell Hart concluded the 1951 text with comments on Rommel's "gifts and performance" that "qualified him for a place in the role [sic] of the 'Great Captains' of history".[629]

Rommel: The Desert Fox

The other foundational text was the influential and laudatory 1950 biography *Rommel: The Desert Fox* by Brigadier Desmond Young.[630,584,631] </ref> Young had served in North Africa in the Indian Army in a public relations capacity, and was once taken prisoner by Rommel's troops.[630] Young interviewed Rommel's widow extensively and collaborated with several individuals who had been close to him, including Hans Speidel, with Liddell Hart also supporting the project. Speidel had already written in 1946 that he planned to turn Rommel into "the hero of the German people", to give them a positive role model. Rommel was a suitable candidate, since the manner of his death had led to the assumption that he had not been a supporter of Nazism. Young subscribed to this view, subtly conveying that Rommel served the regime, but was not part of it.[625,632] The result was predictably positive, "bordering on hagiography", according to the historian Patrick Major.[632,633] </ref>

The reception of *The Desert Fox* in Britain was enthusiastic: the book went through eight editions in a year.[634] Young's biography was another step in the development of the Rommel myth, with Rommel emerging as an active, if not a leading, plotter. Speidel contributed as well, starting from the early 1950s, to bring up Rommel's and his own role in the plot, thus boosting Speidel's suitability for a future role in the new military force of the Federal Republic, the Bundeswehr, and then in NATO.[635]

The book was not without its detractors. The review in *Time* magazine noted the legendary status Rommel had achieved in his lifetime and quoted another review that described Rommel as "the British army's favorite German general." The *Time* reviewer concluded that the book was "just this side of hero worship". Quoting Ernest Bevin, a noted Labour politician, it alluded to the book being an example of the "trade union of generals" in action: Field Marshal Claude Auchinleck, in a foreword to the book, honoured Rommel "as a soldier and a man", and Field Marshal Archibald Wavell included him "among the chosen few, among the very brave, the very true". The reviewer noted the obvious admiration Young had for the German generals, and that the book may well "have been written by [one]".[636] Richard Crossman, a Labour MP, objected to the portrayal of Rommel as an anti-Nazi, writing:[637]

> As a nation, we deceive ourselves into believing that there are two sorts of Germans—the Good German and the Bad German. The "Bad Germans" are Nazis, militarists, anti-democratic, and perpetrators of atrocities. The "Good Germans" are peace-loving democrats and real gentlemen. Ergo, since Rommel was a clean fighter, he must have been anti-Nazi, and men like him would make good allies of democracy against the Russians.

The historian Hugh Trevor-Roper commented that "the danger now is not that 'our friend Rommel' is becoming not a magician or a bogy-man, but too much of a hero". He pointed out Rommel's early proximity to Hitler; he described Rommel as representative of the connection between the Nazism and the Wehrmacht and the support that the German officer corps offered for "Hitler's politics and Hitler's war".[638]

The Desert Fox film

The 1951 film *The Desert Fox: The Story of Rommel*, based on Young's biography, portrayed Rommel in a sympathetic way, as a loyal, humane soldier and a firm opponent to Hitler's policies.[639] The film played up Rommel's disputed role in the conspiracy against Hitler,[640] while omitting Rommel's early association with the dictator.[639]

Writing in *The Daily Telegraph*, under the title "Rommel: A Flattering and Unconvincing Portrait", the journalist Malcolm Muggeridge, who had served in intelligence in North Africa during the war, commented that the film represented "a tendency towards collective schizophrenia whereas ... 'chivalry' towards a captured brigadier is in no wise incompatible with a foreign policy of perfidy and the brutal disregard for all the elementary decencies of civilised behaviour".[637] Critical and public response in the U.S. was muted, but it was a commercial success in Britain, along with a less known 1953 film *The Desert Rats*, where James Mason reprised his portrayal of Rommel.[641]

The film received nearly universally positive reviews in Britain, while protests at the cinemas broke out in Vienna and Milan. Liddell Hart watched the film with a group of high-ranking British officers and reported being "pleasantly surprised".[642,643] </ref> Patrick Major argues that the desert war indeed proved a suitable space to effect the reconciliation among the former enemies. The British popular history focused on that theatre of war, almost to the exclusion of all others. He states that *The Desert Fox* had a "catalytic effect" in creating an image of the German armed forces that would be acceptable to the British public. Rommel was thus successfully integrated into the myth of the clean Wehrmacht.[634]

The Rommel Papers

1953 saw the publication of Rommel's writings of the war period as *The Rommel Papers*, edited by the British journalist and historian B. H. Liddell Hart, the former Wehrmacht officer Fritz Bayerlein, who served on Rommel's staff in North Africa, and Rommel's widow and son. The volume contained an introduction and commentary by Liddell Hart.[644]

The historian Mark Connelly argues that *The Rommel Papers* was one of the two foundational works that lead to a "Rommel renaissance" and "Anglophone rehabilitation", the other being Young's biography.[645] The book contributed to the perception of Rommel as a brilliant commander; in an introduction, Liddell Hart drew comparisons between Rommel and Lawrence of Arabia, "two masters of desert warfare".[646]

Meanwhile, Liddell Hart had a personal interest in the work: by having coaxed Rommel's widow to include material favourable to himself, he could present Rommel as his "pupil" when it came to mobile armoured warfare.[647] Thus, Liddell Hart's "theory of indirect approach" became a precursor to the German *blitzkrieg* ("lightning war"). The controversy was described by the political scientist John Mearsheimer in his work *The Weight of History*, who concluded that, by "putting words in the mouths of German Generals and manipulating history", Liddell Hart was in a position to show that he had been at the root of the dramatic German successes in 1940.[648]

Uncritical accounts

The trend continued with other uncritical biographies, such as *Rommel as Military Commander* (1968), by the former British soldier and author Ronald Lewin, and *Knight's Cross: A Life of Field Marshal Erwin Rommel* (1994), by the former British general David Fraser.[649,650] These works focused on

Rommel's military career, depoliticising it and presenting him strictly as a soldier.[651]

In another work on the North African campaign, the 1977 *The Life and Death of the Africa Korps*, Lewin wrote that it was "necessary to assert that ... the purity of the desert purified the desert war", while Fraser focused on Rommel's battlefield performance and described him as a hero.[651] Fraser's biography remains a work of high reputation,[652,653,654] with Pier Paolo Battistelli praising it for the outstanding handling of the issue of Rommel's myth as well as his life and career in general.[655] However, the work has been criticised by historian Mark Connelly as "encapsulat[ing] the post-1945 hagiographic approach". Connelly offers the example of Fraser's description of Rommel as one of the "great masters of manoeuvre in war", whose personality "transcends time" and "cuts like [a] sabre through the curtains of history".[656]

The historian Patrick Major points out that a recent work, the 2002 book *Alamein: War Without Hate* by Colin Smith and John Bierman, borrowed the name of Rommel's posthumous memoirs for its subtitle.[651] Connelly includes works by Sir John Squire and General Sir John Hackett in the uncritical tradition.[657] In contrast, German biographies, such as by the journalist Wolf Heckmann, were far less sympathetic.[657]

Elements of the myth

According to the historian Mark Connelly, Young and Liddell Hart laid the foundation for the Anglo-American myth, which consisted of three themes: Rommel's ambivalence towards Nazism; his military genius; and the emphasis of the chivalrous nature of the fighting in North Africa.[659] Their works lent support to the image of the "clean Wehrmacht" and were generally not questioned, since they came from British authors, rather than German revisionists.[660,661]</ref> The leading German news magazine *Der Spiegel* describes the myth as "Gentleman warrior, military genius".[662,663]</ref>

According to Watson, the most dominant element in the Rommel myth is Rommel the Superior Soldier, the second being Rommel the Common Man, and the last one Rommel the Martyr.[658] Rosie Goldschmidt Waldeck, writing in 1943, also takes note of the image of the general who fought with common soldiers, with an indelible youthfulness and apparent invulnerability.[664]

Historian Sandra Mass considers the Rommel myth a hero cult, a synthesis of old and new hero cults and traditions culled primarily from Germany's largely imaginary colonial past, in particular the proletarian hero cult originally represented by Carl Peters and the bourgeois one represented by Paul von Lettow-Vorbeck. Rommel, as portrayed by this hero cult, was both chivalrous and

Figure 38: *An iconic picture of Rommel as the "Common Man", helping to free up his staff car alongside his men.*[658]

ruthless, young and old, harsh and gentle, strong and righteous.[665] Calder, Duffy and Ricci opine that Rommel's military brilliance provoked a masochistic tendency to romanticise a worthy opponent, that because he was skilled at his profession, he must have been an anti-Nazi hero.[666,667]

Reevaluation

RecentWikipedia:Manual of Style/Dates and numbers#Chronological items scholarship examined Rommel's attitude towards National Socialism, his performance as a military commander, his role in the 20 July plot and his motivations, leading to a more diverse range of interpretations of Rommel and the elements of the myth.

Relationship with National Socialism

Rommel was not a member of the Nazi Party.[669] However, Rommel, as did other Wehrmacht officers, welcomed Hitler's seizure of power.[670,671] During his time in Goslar, he clashed with those *Sturmabteilung* (SA) men who attacked the Jews and others who supported them. Rommel thus showed sympathy towards Hitler's elimination of the SA, believing the worst was now over,

Figure 39: *Adolf Hitler, accompanied by Rommel, inspects the troops in Goslar, 1934. This was the first meeting between the two men.*[668]

although he opined that in the future the Führer should learn to see his own true strength and refrain from such illegal processes.[672,673] Remy dated Rommel's support for Hitler as 1935, noting a speech in which Rommel praised Hitler for restoring German's self-respect and establishment of the way towards an honourable and righteous peace, as well as efforts in alleviating the disadvantaged people's problems.[672] Numerous historians,Wikipedia:Accuracy dispute#Disputed statement such as Ralf Georg Reuth, David T. Zabecki, Bruce Allen Watson and Peter Caddick-Adams, state that Rommel was one of Hitler's favorite generals and that his close relationship with the dictator benefited both his inter-war and war-time career.[674,675,671] Historian Robert Citino describes Rommel as "not apolitical" and writes that he owed his career to Hitler, to whom his attitude was "worshipful", while the historian Charles Messenger describes Rommel's "growing admiration" towards Hitler following the invasion of Poland.[599,676,677] Peter Caddick-Adams: "As is now clear, Rommel had been very close to Hitler and the Third Reich ..."[678]</ref> Speaking at The National WWII Museum's 2012 International Conference on World War II, the author Nigel Hamilton referred to Rommel as "quite a Nazi".[679] This sympathy did not extend to the Party though. In this regard, he was similar to many other Wehrmacht soldiers, who, with encouragement from Hitler, erroneously believed the army to be the most important element of the regime.[680] Rommel showed particular resentment towards the SA and later, the SS, for

Figure 40: *Rommel, to the right of Hitler, in Poland, September 1939. During the campaign, Rommel enjoyed close proximity to the dictator.*[683]

their brutality and absorption of resources and personnel.[673]

The historian Alaric Searle recasts Rommel's early involvement with the Nazi regime, including his role as a liaison between Hitler Youth and the Wehrmacht. Young's biography had described Rommel's role in strictly military terms and alluded to a falling out between him and the Hitler Youth leader Baldur von Schirach on ideological grounds. In fact, Rommel had twice proposed a plan that would have subordinated Hitler Youth to the army, removing it from the NSDAP control. That went against Schirach's wishes, resulting in Rommel's quiet removal from the project. Searle describes as "patently false" another of Young's assertions, namely that Rommel first became close to Hitler because Hitler had read *Infantry Attacks* and wanted to meet the author in the fall of 1938. This casts doubt on the rest of Young's narrative as it pertains to Rommel's relationship with the dictator.[681] Searle writes that, by this time, "Like many other front-line officers, with little awareness of the military planning underway, Rommel was simply trying to carry out his orders."[681] Remy points out that the incident of Rommel using tanks to protect a journey of Hitler, which has been used by Reuth and Irving to prove that Rommel came to Hitler's attention in 1936, actually happened in 1939. In 1936, according to Remy, Rommel was only a part of the elaborate spectacle that welcomed Hitler, and there was no evidence for the interaction between the two.[682]

Searle argues that Rommel not only "found favor with the Nazi regime, but ... was delighted with the preferential treatment he was receiving", including access to Hitler during the 1939 invasion of Poland. During the campaign, Rommel served as commander of the *Führerbegleitbrigade* battalion, tasked with guarding Hitler and his field headquarters. He attended Hitler's daily war briefings and had opportunities for one-on-one conversations with the dictator, which he proudly reported in letters to his wife. In a sign that he "lost touch with reality", as Searle puts it, Rommel wrote to his wife in October 1939 from the devastated Warsaw, where he was organising a victory parade: "There has been no water, no power, no gas, no food for two days. They have erected numerous barricades which blocked civilian movement and exposed people to bombardments from which they could not escape. The mayor estimated the number of the dead and injured to be 40,000 ... The inhabitants probably drew a breath of relief that we have arrived and rescued them."[683,684]

In 1939, Rommel received a promotion from Hitler to the rank of *Generalmajor* ahead of more senior officers. Showalter notes that even at this early stage, Hitler already regarded Rommel as a model for the fusion of Germany's new and old orders.[685] With an intervention by Hitler, Rommel was subsequently able to obtain command of an armoured (Panzer) division despite having been turned down by the army's personnel office, which had offered him command of a mountain division. Rommel's unprofessional conduct was noted by his fellow officers and added to his growing reputation as one of Hitler's favoured commanders.[671,674] After the Fall of France, Rommel sent to him a specially prepared diary on the 7th Division, Rommel received a letter of thanks.[686] Unknown to Rommel though, Hitler had barely looked at his diary and the letter was written by an adjutant. Remy remarks that by this time, Hitler still did not treat Rommel as a significantly important person.[687]

When Rommel was being considered for appointment as Commander-in-Chief of the Army in the summer of 1942, Goebbels wrote in his diary that Rommel "is ideologically sound, is not just sympathetic to the National Socialists. He is a National Socialist; he is a troop leader with a gift for improvisation, personally courageous and extraordinarily inventive. These are the kinds of soldiers we need."[675]

Rommel "exercised an almost hypnotic influence on Hitler", according to Albert Kesselring,[689] and another colleague called him "the Führer's marshal". American writer Rick Atkinson concludes that Rommel was "loyal in his own fashion and as beguiled by Hitler as steel filings by a magnet ... Hitler was a bulwark against bolshevism, [Rommel] had told staff officers."[688] Despite this intimate relationship though, he was not provided with basic information on Germany's strategic plan: "Rommel did not know that smashing the Soviet Union and major territorial acquisitions in the East would be the cornerstone

Figure 41: *Rommel and Hitler in 1942. According to Rick Atkinson, Rommel was known as "the Führer's marshal".*[688]

of this plan. Nor did Rommel realise that Hitler saw no conflict of interest between Germany and the maritime power Great Britain, which he hoped to make an ally."[690] He also had only a week's warning before the launch of Case White at the start of 1943.[691] Messenger argues that Rommel's attitude towards Hitler changed only after the Allied invasion of Normandy, when Rommel came to realise that the war could not be won.[676]

Historian Thomas Vogel opines that Rommel was not a Nazi, if one uses the definition the Nazis themselves used, considering that although he did everything in his power to make his country strong again, he showed no support towards the racial policies or other aspects of the regime.

Operational and strategic level commander

British military and political figures contributed to the heroic image of the man as Rommel resumed offensive operations in January 1942 against the British forces weakened by redeployments to the Far East. Speaking in the House of Commons, Churchill addressed the British defeats and described Rommel as an "extraordinary bold and clever opponent" and a "great field commander".[605,606] The trend continued after the war following the publication of *The Desert Fox*, which also portrays staff officers like Wilhelm Keitel, Alfred Jodl and Franz Halder, who opposed Rommel on strategic issues, as having ulterior motives in smearing him (Simon Ball also notes that this was the single group of people in the postwar West who had an interest in denigrating Rommel, who had never been one of them).[581,692] Former military opponents in

Britain described Rommel as a brilliant commander and a resistance fighter, the "good German", with one senior military figure comparing Rommel to legendary military leader Belisarius. The praise led Bernard Montgomery's former deputy, Brian Horrocks, to argue in his 1950 article "The Rommel Myth Debunked" that the Eighth Army beat Rommel's Afrika Korps "fair and square".[583] In 1977, Martin van Creveld started the reevaluation of Malta's impact on supply situations[693] and concluded that Rommel was largely responsible for his supply problems (caused by overextended supply lines which prevented the Afrika Korps from receiving the supplies that the Italians were able to provide in adequate numbers). According to Creveld, the capacity of Libyan ports were too small and the distances to be overcome too great for Rommel to advance a more ambitious plan than Hitler's original one of defending a limited area.[694]

Certain modern historians, such as Larry T. Addington, Niall Barr and Robert Citino, are skeptical of Rommel as an operational, let alone strategic, level commander. They point to Rommel's lack of appreciation for Germany's strategic situation, his misunderstanding of the relative importance of his theatre to the German High Command, his poor grasp of logistical realities, and, according to the historian Ian Beckett, his "penchant for glory hunting".[695,599] Citino credits Rommel's limitations as an operational level commander as "materially contributing" to the eventual demise of the Axis forces in North Africa,[599,696]</ref> Meanwhile Addington focuses on Rommel's disobedience and struggle over the North Africa strategy, whereby his initial brilliant success resulted in "catastrophic effects" for Germany in this theatre of war.[697]

The historian Geoffrey P. Megargee refers to Rommel as a "talented tactical leader", but points out his playing the German and Italian command structures against each other to his advantage. Rommel used the confused structure of the OKW (Supreme Command of the Wehrmacht), the OKH (Supreme High Command of the Army) and the Italian Supreme Command to disregard orders that he disagreed with or to appeal to whatever authority he felt would be most sympathetic to his requests.[698] Rommel often went directly to Hitler with his needs and concerns, taking advantage of the favoritism that the Führer displayed towards him and adding to the German High Command's distrust of him.[699]

Military practitioners have also questioned Rommel's abilities at the operational level. While nearly all acknowledge Rommel's excellent tactical skills and personal bravery, many officers came to accept that Rommel was "possibly the most overrated commander of an army in world history", writes U.S. major general and military historian David T. Zabecki of the United States Naval Institute, quoting the opinion of Wolf Heckmann. Zabecki notes that Rommel's brilliant tactical moves were logistically unsustainable, which eventually led to a strategic defeat.[674,700]</ref> General Klaus Naumann, who served as Chief of Staff of the Bundeswehr, agrees with Charles Messenger that Rommel had challenges on the operational level, and states that Rommel's violation of the unity of command principle, bypassing the chain of command in Africa, was unacceptable.[701,702]</ref>

Some historians, such as Zabecki and Peter Lieb, also take issue with Rommel's absence from Normandy on the day of the Allied invasion, 6 June 1944. He had left France on 5 June and was at home on the 6th celebrating his wife's birthday. Rommel either planned or claimed to have planned to proceed to see Hitler the next day to discuss the situation in Normandy.[703,704] Zabecki calls his decision to leave the theatre in view of an imminent invasion "an incredible lapse of command responsibility".[703]

More sympathetic authors point out complex situations that Rommel had to face. Brian Hanley, from USNI's Editorial Board of Directors, comments that Rommel was beaten the moment he arrived in Africa, considering the Allied troops outnumbered the Afrika Korps and they worked under a much more straightforward chain of command, while orders sent from Berlin to North Africa were rarely kept confidential. Hanley sees Rommel turning German and Italian military authorities against each other as turning liabilities into advantages and that he repeatedly created operational miracles that made a strategic investment in the Africa theatre attractive in 1942. Also, according to Hanley, if Rommel stood still, his enemy's strength would accumulate while his own, depending on an uncertain supply line, would diminish, thus he needed the British stocks of supply to deal with his logistical problems.[705]

Samuel W. Mitcham points out that Rommel's German forces in Africa were so outnumbered that if the outcome was ever in question, it was the true measure of his genius.[706] Mitcham recognises Rommel more as "a master of mobile warfare", but opines that by the Invasion of Normandy in 1944, he had developed "a cunning sense of strategy".[707] Daniel Allen Butler writes that if Rommel was not a formally trained strategist, he developed himself into one, becoming able to grasp strategic opportunities that others missed. Starting as a compulsive commander who imperiled his own command, and his superiors' plans in Africa, he realized that his opponent's army was the main objective and not the mere holding of territory. Butler writes that it was unfair to blame Rommel considering that he had been kept ignorant of Operation Barbarossa. Butler also questions the need to obey his superiors' higher strategy, considering that Hitler never had a coherent grand strategy.[708]

Others like Stroud, Krause and Phillips opine that even Rommel's recklessness and disobedience during the invasion of France benefitted the German cause, while rescuing Hitler's mercurial objectives and inventing the actual application of *blitzkrieg* ("lightning war"), and it was Hitler who downgraded strategic victory to operational victory.[709,710] According to Alan J. Levine, contrary to the allegation that he was only a genius tactician without a good grasp of logistics, Rommel was a clearer thinker than most of his colleagues (shown by his judgements on developing situations), and although he was the most defeatist German general, there was a serious qualification to his pessimism and he was capable of displaying a surprising amount of energy in building the Normandy defense at the same time.[711]

MacGregor Knox, whose works draw largely on Italian sources, opines that rather than technical and expertise weaknesses, effectiveness in war ultimately depends on culture, the command style and ethos, which in turn breed technological imagination and force structure. He points out that the few Italian mobile units fighting together with the Afrika Korps benefitted from working under Rommel, who helped them cope with rapidly changing situations in a war without fixed fronts, despite interference from Ettore Bastico.[712] Marvin Knorr expresses a sympathetic view of Rommel's attitude to the General Staff, saying that their attitudes towards officers of middle class like him made it understandable that he was wary about them, and worried that the officers they sent to him would report on him or try to take over. Despite this, he came to trust and depend on these staff officers, like Friedrich von Mellenthin and Siegfried Westphal, who in turn proved their talent and loyalty.[713] Rick Atkinson acknowledges Rommel's "audacity, tactical brilliance, and personal style", also noting that he "had an uncanny ability to dominate the minds of his adversaries".[714]

Some authors like Boog and Lewin opine that while Creveld's statistics regarding the losses of supplies are not wrong and that the vast distances were a big problem, the failure of the seaborne supply lines was still a deciding factor because operationally effective supplies often failed to arrive at decisive moments of the campaigns.[715,716] Douglas Austin points out that the overall port capacity at Tobruk and Benghazi was actually sufficient and that the recently published Enigma intercepts show that it was the bulk losses at sea (and not unloading or getting the supplies to forward areas) that had the greater impact on Rommel's decisions as well as those of other German commanders, like Kesselring.[717] Levine dismisses poor port capacity and lack of transport vehicles as the Afrika Korps' crucial weaknesses, citing evidences gathered on British intelligence by Hinsley and Bennett.[718] Others point out Rommel's dependence on captured resources as compensation for the unstable supply lines and unfulfilled promises (by 1942, 85% of his transport were captured vehicles).[719,720,721] Butler opines that the myth of Rommel's bad logistical management is the result of rumours started by Halder.[720]

Role in 20 July plot

The extent of Rommel's involvement in the military's resistance against Hitler or the 20 July plot is difficult to ascertain, as people most directly involved did not survive, and limited documentation of the conspirators' plans and preparations exists. Thus, Rommel's participation remains ambiguous, and the perception of it largely has its source in subsequent events (especially Rommel's forced suicide) and the post-war accounts by surviving participants.[722]

According to a post-war account by Karl Strölin, the *Oberbürgermeister* of Stuttgart at that time, he and two other conspirators, Alexander von Falkenhausen and Carl Heinrich von Stülpnagel, began efforts to bring Rommel into the anti-Hitler conspiracy in early 1944.[723] On 15 April 1944, Rommel's new chief of staff, Hans Speidel, arrived in Normandy and reintroduced Rommel to Stülpnagel.[724] Speidel had previously been connected to Carl Goerdeler, the civilian leader of the resistance, but not to the plotters led by Stauffenberg, and only came to the attention of Stauffenberg due to his appointment to Rommel's headquarters. The conspirators felt they needed the support of a field marshal on active duty, and gave instructions to Speidel to bring Rommel into their circle.[725]

Speidel met with former foreign minister Konstantin von Neurath and Strölin on 27 May in Germany, ostensibly at Rommel's request, although the latter was not present. Neurath and Strölin suggested opening immediate surrender negotiations with the West, and, according to Speidel, Rommel agreed to further discussions and preparations.[726] However, around the same time the plotters in Berlin were not aware that Rommel had reportedly decided to take part in the conspiracy. On 16 May, they informed Allen Dulles, through whom they hoped to negotiate with the Western Allies, that Rommel could not be counted on for support.[727]

Rommel opposed assassinating Hitler. After the war, his widow maintained that Rommel believed an assassination attempt would spark a civil war.[728] Historian Ian Beckett argues that "there is no credible evidence that Rommel had more than limited and superficial knowledge of the plot" and concludes that Rommel would not have acted to aid the plotters on 20 July,[722] while Ralf Georg Reuth contends that "there was no indication of any active participation of Rommel in the conspiracy".[729] Historian Richard J. Evans concluded that he knew of a plot, but was not involved.[730]

What is not debated are the results of the failed bomb plot of 20 July. Many conspirators were arrested, and the dragnet expanded to thousands.[731] Consequently, it did not take long for Rommel to come under suspicion, beginning with evidence the SS obtained from Stülpnagel who mentioned Rommel in delirium after his failed suicide.[732,733,734] Rommel's name also came up in confessions by Stülpnagel's personal adviser, Caesar von Hofacker, and was included in Goerdeler's papers on a list of potential supporters.[735,736] The author and cinematographer Maurice Philip Remy discovered a memo from Martin Bormann, the head of the Nazi Party Chancellery, dating from 28 September 1944 in which the Chief of the Party Chancellery, and Personal Secretary to Hitler, stated that "former General Stülpnagel, former Colonel Hofacker, Kluge's meanwhile executed nephew Lieutenant-Colonel Rathgens and other defendants still alive gave all testimony that Field-Marshal Rommel was indeed in the picture; Rommel agreed that he would be at the new government's disposal after a successful plot".[737]

According to eavesdropped conversations between German generals in British captivity, edited by the historian Sönke Neitzel, the former commander of the 5th Panzer Army, General Heinrich Eberbach, claimed on 14 September 1944 that Rommel had told him in Normandy, just a few days before the plot, that Hitler and his entourage would have to be killed, if there was any chance for Germany to bring the war to a satisfactory end.[738] Summarising the most recent findings on Rommel's role in the 20 July plot, Peter Lieb concludes that Rommel

> *did not play any role in the operational preparations for the plot against Hitler and we do not know which post he was supposed to assume after a successful coup. Hence, the Field-Marshal was definitely not part of the most inner circle of the 20 July plotters. At the same time, however, he was more than just a mere sympathiser and paid for this with his life. He consequently deserves a firm place in the military resistance against Hitler to a greater extent than it has recently been acknowledged in academia and in public.*[739]

Analysis of motivations

Rommel was an ambitious man who took advantage of his proximity to Hitler and willingly accepted the propaganda campaigns designed for him by Goebbels.[670] He sought to level the playing field for non-nobles, and also supported militarism and a strong German Empire,[740,741] while treating people only according to their merits.[742] He did not display hatred to people of noble descent, and in fact was a throwback to the medieval knight in his personal traits, appearing well-versed in the ancient customs of chivalry,[743,744] which helped to attract admiration from the British who saw in him a romantic archetype.[745] Rommel classed himself as a traditionalist regarding military ethics and a modernist regarding warfare techniques.[746] Certain authors remark that he also sought military glory and personal recognition, most of all from Hitler on whom, according to Watson, Rommel projected his idea of the German people's will.[740,747]</ref>

Figure 42: *Rommel posing for a propaganda photo in North Africa. According to Klaus Naumann, "Rommel was used by the Nazi regime to create a myth. He tolerated this since he had a strong dose of personal ambition and vanity.*"[670]

A number of contemporaries noted Rommel's vanity. In the memorandum regarding Rommel's betrayal, Martin Bormann remarked, "He had himself photographed from dawn to dusk ... He is so vain he does not wear glasses". (Rommel was near-sighted in one eye and far-sighted in the other.)[748] Some modern authors, such as Storbeck, are more sympathetic. He states that Rommel's perceived vanity developed as a reaction to the pressure aristocratic and high-bourgeois colleagues put on him. The psychologist Norman F. Dixon remarks that although Rommel showed towards Hitler an admiration that later faded, he did not display the urge to submit himself to higher authority or powerful father figures, considering that had he been such a person, he would not have been so outspoken or risked himself in the struggle against people like Himmler, Keitel or Jodl.[749]

Messenger points out that Rommel had many reasons to be grateful to Hitler, including his interference to arrange for him to receive command of an armoured division, his elevation to the status of a national hero, and continued interest and support from the dictator. Remy states that the attachment to Hitler went much deeper than any gratefulness could explain, and that Hitler had become Rommel's source of motivation.[750] Some, like Randall Hansen,[751] highlight the similarities in background and personality that facilitated the rapport between the two, while others, like Richard Overy, state that Rommel's main appeal to Hitler was that he was everything Hitler was not,[752] while the political scientist Roland Detsch, in a review of Maurice Remy's book, comments that despite Remy's efforts, the strange relationship remains hard to understand.[753] Wolfram Pyta remarks that Hitler did not compete with Rommel for the war leader image because the two complemented each other perfectly. They were similar in the sense that they were the only ones with a cultural presence and objects around whom German society's grand narrative was being built, thus Rommel was the only German general who would have been capable of challenging Hitler's rule, had he ever crossed the Rubicon from his "apolitical-to-the-core" military world and developed a serious, critical view of Hitler's political dealings. However, Rommel himself had fallen for Hitler's charisma almost until the end.[754]

Caddick-Adams writes that Rommel was a "complicated man of many contradictions",[498] while Beckett notes that "Rommel's myth ... has proved remarkably resilient" and that more work is needed to put him in proper historical context.[722] Zabecki concludes that "the blind hero worship ... only distorts the real lessons to be learned from [his] career and battles",[674] and Watson notes that the legend has been a "distraction" that obscured the evolution of Rommel as a military commander and his changing attitudes towards the regime that he served.[755]

John Pimlott writes that Rommel was an impressive military commander who richly deserved his reputation as a leading exponent of mobile warfare, hampered by factors he could not control, although he usually accepted high risks and could become frustrated when forced on the defensive. On the other hand, Pimlott criticises Rommel for only disagreeing with Hitler for strategic reasons and, while accepting that Rommel did give chivalrous tone to his battles in Africa, he points out that this should not be used to ignore the responsibility Rommel must bear for promoting the Nazi cause with vigour.[756] The same sentiment is held by Murray and Millett who opine that Rommel, contrary to allegations that he was only a competent tactical commander, was the most outstanding battlefield commander of the war, who showed a realistic strategic view despite holding minimal control over strategy. They point out that, "like virtually the entire German officer corps", he was a convinced Nazi.[757]

Cornelia Hecht, the author of the 2008 exhibition named *Mythos Rommel* and a book of the same name, explains that despite extensive research, it is hard to see who Rommel really was under all the layers of the myth. She comments that she would not describe Rommel as a resistance fighter, although he did support the assassination attempt. Patrick Major describes Rommel as someone who went along with the regime as long as it served his needs, a "fellow traveler rather than a war criminal".[758] Summing up Rommel's career in a 2012 interview with Reuters, the historian Sönke Neitzel states:[640]

> On the one hand he didn't commit war crimes that we know of and ordered a retreat at El Alamein despite Hitler's order. But he took huge German casualties elsewhere and he was a servant of the regime. He was not exactly a shining liberal or Social Democrat. Mostly, he was interested in his career.

Historian Reuth observes that the modern German image of Rommel (a result of the *Historikerstreit* in the 1980s and debates on war guilt during the 1990s), as represented most notably by Maurice Rémy, is that of both a National Socialist and a hero of the Resistance. Reuth argues that "Rommel was neither one nor the other. He had understood neither National Socialism, nor the resistance to it. Like millions of Germans he followed Hitler into disaster and whilst doing so he believed he was only doing his duty."[759]

Historiography

Although the author David Irving and his works have now become controversial for his denial of the Holocaust, he is recognised as the historian who started the re-evaluation of Rommel. He was the first historian to gain access to a large number of Rommel's private letters, and his well-substantiated findings questioned Rommel's image as a "chivalrous resistance fighter". This biography, however, has been criticized by other authors like Mitcham, Dowe and Hecht for misrepresentation of the subject[760] or manipulation and misrepresentation of primary sources, and even invention of verbatim quotations with the aim of portraying Hitler in a better light.[761]

Works such as the 2002 documentary *Mythos Rommel* by Remy, and the book of the same name, and the 2004 book *Rommel: Das Ende einer Legende* (published in English in 2005 as *Rommel: The End of a Legend*) by German historian Ralf Georg Reuth, furthered the discussion on both Rommel and his myth.[584] In the continued debate on Rommel and his legacy, Christopher Gabel criticises the documentary *Rommel's War* (made by historians Jörg Müllner and Jean-Christoph Caron) for using false analogy to prove that Rommel was a war criminal by association, without providing any evidence even of Rommel's knowledge about crimes in his areas of operation.[762] According to Matthias Stickler, attacks on Rommel's integrity and attempts to link him to war crimes, which were started by the "journalist side" in the 1990s, have been largely repudiated by serious research despite having been repeatedly rehashed and refreshed by some authors and their epigones. Stickler gives recognition to both Remy and Reuth for offering possible explanations for Rommel's character evolution.[763]

Numerous English-speaking authors use the "Rommel Myth" ambiguously, like Bruce Allen Watson who states that "the masks he wore reflected the genuine plurality of the man",[764] or Jill Edwards, who notes that, below all the layers historians have removed and added to, what remains seems enough to qualify Rommel as, if controversial, a great captain.[765] Others who mention and depict the myth as a phenomenon that is either hard to ascertain or has a core that reflects reality include Pier Paolo Battistelli,[766]</ref> Randall Hansen,[767] Ian Baxter,[768] T.L. McMahon,[769] Brighton,[770] Rosie Goldschmidt Waldeck,[664] Mitcham,[771] Charles F. Marshall,[772] Majdalany,[773] Latimer,[774] and Showalter.[775]

A German author who uses the word *Mythos* in a critical manner is Ralph Giordano,[776]</ref> who describes the phenomenon as one of the "Falsehoods of Tradition" in his book of the same name, which depicts how the image of Rommel has been a major basis for the warrior cult of the Bundeswehr.[777] Sir David Hunt describes himself as being critical towards the Rommel mythology. While he has "the highest praise for his character", his impression of Rommel as a commander is a dashing cavalryman who gambled deep and lost in the end. Other authors who present popular narratives on Rommel as a misguided or deliberately falsified myth include James Sadkovich, who criticises both Rommel's supposed genius and his treatment of his Italian allies,[778] and: James Robinson,[596] Martin Kitchen,[779] Alaric Searle,[650] Robert Citino,[780] Ralf Georg Reuth,[598] Kenneth Macksey.[781]

Controversies over modern role as the Bundeswehr's role model

Numerous critics take issue with the Bundeswehr's reverence towards Rommel as its primary role model.[783,784,785,786,782,787,788] While recognizing his great talents as a commander, they point out several problems like Rommel's involvement with a criminal regime, his political naivete, or that he can not teach the society modern values like democracy, pacifism, critical thinking or feminism. The politician scientist Ralph Rotte calls for his replacement with Manfred von Richthofen.[784] Cornelia Hecht opines that whatever judgement history will pass on Rommel – who was the idol of World War II as well as the integration figure of the post-war Republic – it is now the time the Bundeswehr should rely on its own history and tradition and not any Wehrmacht commander.[789] Jürgen Heiducoff, a retired Bundeswehr officer, writes that the maintenance of the Rommel barracks' names and the definition of Rommel as a resistance fighter are capitulation before neo-Nazi tendencies. Heiducoff agrees with Bundeswehr generals that Rommel was one of the greatest strategists and tacticians, both in theory and practice, and a victim of contemporary

Figure 43: *The Field Marshal Rommel Barracks' exercise field with the Teutoburg Forest, usually affiliated with Arminius, in the background. Critics note that the blend of the two figures represented by the placing of a Rommel portrait and an Arminius statue together in the main building, seems to combine Germanic cults, with veneration towards the Wehrmacht.*[782]

jealous colleagues, but argues that such a talent for aggressive, destructive warfare is not a suitable model for the Bundeswehr, a primarily defensive army. Heiducoff criticizes Bundeswehr generals for pressuring the Ministry of Defence into making decisions in favour of the man they openly admire.[786] The Green Party's position is that Rommel was not a war criminal but still had entanglements with war crimes, and that he could not be the Bundeswehr's role model.[790,782]

Historian Michael Wolffsohn supports the Ministry of Defense's decision to continue recognition of Rommel, although he thinks the focus should be put on the later stage of Rommel's life, when he began thinking more seriously about war and politics, and broke with the regime. MDR reports that, "Wolffsohn declares the Bundeswehr wants to have politically thoughtful, responsible officers from the beginning, thus a tradition of 'swashbuckler' and 'humane rescuer' is not intended".[791] According to authors like Ulrich vom Hagen and Sandra Mass though, the Bundeswehr (as well as NATO) deliberately endorses the ideas of chivalrous warfare and apolitical soldiering associated with Rommel.[792,588,793] According to Cornelia Hecht, the Bundeswehr believes that "chivalry and fairness", which Rommel embodied more than any other

Wehrmacht generals, are timeless military virtues.[789,794] At a Ministry conference soliciting input on the matter, Dutch general Ton van Loon advised the Ministry that, although there can be historical abuses hidden under the guise of military tradition, tradition is still essential for the *esprit de corps* and part of that tradition should be the leadership and achievements of Rommel.[795]

The Field Marshal Rommel Barracks, Augustdorf stresses his leadership and performance as worthy of tradition and identity, establishing, among other things, no proven war crime as a reason to keep the name.[782] The Sanitary Regiment 3, stationed at the Rommel Barracks in Dornstadt, also desires (almost unanimously, as revealed by an interdepartmental opinion poll) to keep the name.[796] The Parliamentary Commissioner for the Armed Forces Hans Peter Bartels (SPD) supports the keeping of the name and the tradition associated with Rommel, but notes that the reasons should not be his initial successes in Africa, or that the former adversary armies have continued to worship him until this day. Bartels adds that Rommel, who probably supported the Resistance, is a borderline case regarding which historians find it hard to ascertain, and German history is full of such ambiguities.[797,798] In early 2017, German Federal Ministry of Defence, in response to a petition championed by historian Wolfgang Proske and backed by politicians from the Left Party, defended the naming of barracks after Rommel, with the justification that the current state of research does not support their allegations. The political scientist and politician Alexander Neu criticizes the Ministry's undeterred attitude to the fact Rommel was at least near-Nazi and did serve the unjust regime, and comments that the association of Rommel with the spirit of the Bundeswehr is not new, but they did not expect that the Federal Ministry of Defence, without providing at least a bibliography, would declare him a victim of the regime as well.[799]

References

Informational notes

Citations

Bibliography <templatestyles src="Template:Refbegin/styles.css" />
- "Armored Knight". *Time*. **57** (4): 100. 1951.
- Addington, Larry H. (1967). "Operation Sunflower: Rommel Versus the General Staff"[800]. *Military Affairs*. **31** (3): 120.
- Arquilla, John (1996). *From Troy to Entebbe: Special Operations in Ancient and Modern Times*[801]. University Press of America. p. 218. ISBN 978-0-7618-0186-3.
- Atkinson, Rick (2002). *An Army at Dawn*. New York: Picador. ISBN 978-0-8050-8724-6.

- Atkinson, Rick (2013). *The Guns at Last Light*. New York: Henry Holt. ISBN 978-0-8050-6290-8.
- Austin, Douglas (2004). *Malta and British Strategic Policy, 1925-43*[802]. Routledge. p. 20. ISBN 9781135769383.
- Ball, Simon (17 August 2016). *Alamein: Great Battles*[803]. Oxford University Press,. ISBN 978-0-19-150462-4.
- Barnett, Correlli (1989). *Hitler's Generals*[804]. Grove Press. ISBN 0-8021-3994-9.
- Barr, Niall (2014). "Rommel in the Desert, 1941". In I. F. W. Beckett. *Rommel Reconsidered*. Mechanicsburg, PA: Stackpole Books. ISBN 978-0-8117-1462-4.
- Bartels, Hans-Peter (19 November 2017). "Kein Pomp. Keine Helden. Nirgends Pracht"[805]. die Welt. Retrieved 8 April 2018.
- Battistelli, Pier Paolo (2012). *Erwin Rommel*[806]. Bloomsbury Publishing. ISBN 978-1-78096-471-3.
- Baxter, Ian (2014). *Afrika Korps*[807]. Pen and Sword. ISBN 978-1-84415-683-2.
- Beckett, Ian (2014). "Introduction". In I. F. W. Beckett. *Rommel Reconsidered*. Mechanicsburg, PA: Stackpole Books. ISBN 978-0-8117-1462-4.
- Beevor, Antony (2012). *The Second World War*. New York: Back Bay Books. ISBN 978-0-316-02374-0.
- Blumenson, Martin (2001). *Heroes Never Die: Warriors and Warfare in World War II*. Cooper Square Press. ISBN 978-0-8154-1152-9.
- Böhmer, Willi (6 November 2012). "Rommelkaserne umtaufen"[808]. SÜDWEST PRESSE. Retrieved 21 August 2017.
- Boog, Horst; Rahn, Werner; Stumpf, Reinhard; Wegner, Bernd (2001). *Germany and the Second World War: Volume 6: The Global War*[809]. OUP Oxford. p. 839. ISBN 9780191606847.
- Brighton, Terry (2008). *Masters of Battle: Monty, Patton and Rommel at War*[810]. New York: Viking. ISBN 978-0-670-91691-7.
- Brighton, Terry (2009). *Patton, Montgomery, Rommel: Masters of War*. Crown/Archetype. ISBN 978-1-4001-1497-9.
- Butler, Daniel Allen (2015). *Field Marshal: The Life and Death of Erwin Rommel*[811]. Havertown, PA / Oxford: Casemate. ISBN 978-1-61200-297-2.
- Caddick-Adams, Peter (2012). *Monty and Rommel: Parallel Lives*. New York, NY: The Overlook Press. ISBN 978-1-59020-725-3.
- Calder, Angus (2012). *The People's War: Britain 1939–1945*[812]. Random House. pp. 242, 265, 304, 524, 564. ISBN 978-1-4481-0310-2.
- Ceva, Lucio (1990). "The North African Campaign, 1940–43: A Reconsideration". In John Gooch. *Decisive Campaigns of the Second World*

- *War*. Abingdon: Taylor & Francis. ISBN 978-0-7146-3369-5.
- Chambers, Madeline (2012). "The Devil's General? German film seeks to debunk Rommel myth"[813]. *Reuters*. Archived[814] from the original on 11 December 2016. Retrieved 8 February 2016.
- Citino, Robert (2007). *Death of the Wehrmacht: The German Campaigns of 1942*[815]. University Press of Kansas. Archived from the original[816] on 6 October 2016.
- Citino, Robert (2012). "Rommel's Afrika Korps"[817]. *HistoryNet*. Archived[818] from the original on 11 December 2016. Retrieved 3 March 2016.
- Coetzee, Daniel (2013). *Philosophers of War: The Evolution of History's Greatest Military Thinkers*[819]. ABC-CLIO. ISBN 978-0-313-07033-4.
- Connelly, Mark (2014). "Rommel as icon". In I. F. W. Beckett. *Rommel Reconsidered*. Mechanicsburg, PA: Stackpole Books. ISBN 978-0-8117-1462-4.
- Connelly, Owen (2009). *On War and Leadership: The Words of Combat Commanders from Frederick the Great to Norman Schwarzkopf*. Princeton: Princeton University Press. ISBN 978-1-4008-2516-5.
- Creveld, Martin van (1977). *Supplying War: Logistics from Wallenstein to Patton*. Cambridge: Cambridge University Press. ISBN 0-521-21730-X.
- Däniker, Gustav; Keren, Michael; Sylvan, Donald A. (2002). *International Intervention: Sovereignty Versus Responsibility*[820]. Psychology Press. p. 117. ISBN 978-0-7146-5192-7.
- Detsch, Roland (2002). "Die andere Wahrheit"[821]. *context politik: wissenschaft: kultur*. Archived[822] from the original on 11 December 2016. Retrieved 30 May 2016.
- Deuel, Wallace R. (1943). *A 'Model' Teuton; MEET MR. BLANK. By R.G. Waldeck. 179 pp. New York: G.P. Putnam's Boris. $2.50. Mr. Blank – The Model Teuton (The New York Times Book Review, Volume 2)*[823]. Arno Press. Retrieved 14 September 2017.
- Dixon, Norman F. (2016). *On the Psychology of Military Incompetence*[824]. Basic Books. ISBN 978-0-465-09780-7.
- Dowe, Christopher; Hecht, Cornelia (2016). "Von Mythen, Legenden und Manipulationen. David Irving und seine verzerrende Deutungen von Erwin Rommel, Hans Speidel und Cäsar von Hofacker". In Haus der Geschichte Baden-Württemberg. *Verräter? Vorbilder? Verbrecher? Kontroverse Deutungen des 20. Juli 1944 seit 1945*. Frank & Timme GmbH. p. 129–160. ISBN 9783732902767.
- Duffy, James P.; Ricci, Vincent L. (2013). *Target Hitler: The Many Plots to Kill Adolf Hitler*[825]. Enigma Books. ISBN 978-1-936274-03-1.

- Echternkamp, Jörg (2010). *Die 101 wichtigsten Fragen – der Zweite Weltkrieg*[826]. C. H. Beck. ISBN 978-3-406-59314-7.
- Edwards, Jill (2012). *El Alamein and the Struggle for North Africa: International Perspectives from the Twenty-first Century*[827]. Oxford University Press. ISBN 978-977-416-581-8.
- Evans, Richard J. (2009). *The Third Reich at War*. New York: Penguin. ISBN 978-0-14-101548-4.
- FAZ (28 March 2018). "„Geht nicht darum, alle Erinnerungsstücke wegzuräumen""[828]. Frankfurter Allgemeine Zeitung. Retrieved 8 April 2018.
- Fischer, Thomas (2014). "Rommel und Hitler"[829]. *SWR*. Retrieved 30 May 2016.
- Fraser, David (1993). *Knight's Cross: A Life of Field Marshal Erwin Rommel*[830]. New York: HarperCollins. Retrieved 23 April 2016.
- Friedmann, Jan (23 May 2007). "World War II: New Research Taints Image of Desert Fox Rommel"[831]. *Spiegel Online*. Archived from the original[832] on 11 December 2016. Retrieved 4 March 2016.
- Gabel, Christopher (2014). *Great Commanders [Illustrated Edition]*. Pickle Partners Publishing. ISBN 978-1-78289-446-9.
- Giordano, Ralph (2000). *Die Traditionslüge: vom Kriegerkult in der Bundeswehr*[833]. Kiepenheuer & Witsch. ISBN 978-3-462-02921-5.
- Giordano, Ralph (2010). *Mein Leben ist so sündhaft lang: ein Tagebuch*[834]. Kiepenheuer & Witsch. ISBN 978-3-462-04240-5.
- Goldschmidt Waldeck, Rosie (1943). *Meet Mr. Blank: The Leader of Tomorrow's Germans*[835]. G. P. Putnam's sons.
- Hachten Wee, Patricia; Wee, Robert James (2004). *World War II in Literature for Youth: A Guide and Resource Book*[836]. Scarecrow Press. ISBN 978-0-8108-5301-0.
- Hagen, Ulrich vom (2014). *Homo militaris: Perspektiven einer kritischen Militärsoziologie*[837]. Verlag (transcript). ISBN 978-3-8394-1937-3.
- Hamilton, Nigel (2012). "Defeating the Desert Fox"[838]. *The National WWII Museum*. Retrieved 8 October 2016.
- Hanley, Brian (2008). *Planning for Conflict in the Twenty-first Century*[839]. Greenwood Publishing Group. ISBN 978-0-313-34555-5.
- Hansen, Randall (2014). *Disobeying Hitler: German Resistance After Valkyrie*[840]. New York: Oxford University Press. ISBN 978-0-19-992792-0.
- Hart, Russel A. (2014). "Rommel and the 20th July Bomb Plot". In F. W. Beckett. *Rommel Reconsidered*. Mechanicsburg, PA: Stackpole Books. ISBN 978-0-8117-1462-4.
- Hartmann, Bernd (2011). *Panzers in the Sand: The History of Panzer-Regiment 5, 1942-45, Volume 2*[841]. Stackpole Books. p. 138.

ISBN 9780811744324.
- Hecht (editor), Cornelia; Häussler, Johannes; Linder, Rainer (2008). *Mythos Rommel*. Haus der Geschichte Baden-Württemberg. ISBN 978-3-933726-28-5.
- Heiducoff, Jürgen (20 August 2017). "Kapitulation vor neonazistischen Realitäten"[842]. NRhZ-Online - Neue Rheinische Zeitung. Retrieved 20 August 2017.
- Holles, Everett (1945). *Unconditional Surrender*[843]. Howell, Soskin. p. 227.
- Kanold, Jurgen (2012). "Denkmal des Anstoßes"[844]. Retrieved 2016-08-04.
- Kanold, Jürgen (19 May 2017). "Bundeswehr: Verminte Geschichte"[845]. SÜDWEST PRESSE. Retrieved 20 August 2017.
- Knab, Jakob (1999). "Verklärung und Aufklärung Von den Heldenmythen der Wehrmacht zur Traditionspflege der Bundeswehr"[846] (PDF). *Vierteljahresschrift für Sicherheit und Friede* (2/1999). Retrieved 20 August 2017.
- Knab, Jakob (19 May 2017). "Traditionspflege ist eine wertende Auswahl"[847] (PDF). Die Tagespost. Retrieved 19 August 2017.
- Kitchen, Martin (2009). *Rommel's Desert War: Waging World War II in North Africa, 1941–1943*. Cambridge University Press. ISBN 978-0-521-50971-8.
- Kitchen, Martin (14 January 2014). *A World in Flames: A Short History of the Second World War in Europe and Asia 1939–1945*[848]. Routledge,. p. 84. ISBN 978-1-317-90094-8.
- Knopp, Guido (2013). *Hitlers Krieger*[849]. C. Bertelsmann Verlag. ISBN 978-3-641-11998-0.
- Knorr Jr., Major Marvin (2015). *The Development Of German Doctrine And Command And Control And Its Application To Supporting Arms, 1832–1945*[850]. Pickle Partners Publishing. ISBN 978-1-78625-062-9.
- Knox, MacGregor (2000). *Hitler's Italian Allies: Royal Armed Forces, Fascist Regime, and the War of 1940–1943*[851]. Cambridge University Press. ISBN 978-1-139-43203-0.
- Krause, Michael D.; Phillips, R. Cody (2006). *Historical Perspectives of the Operational Art*[852]. Government Printing Office. ISBN 978-0-16-072564-7.
- Kubetzky, Thomas (2010). *'The mask of command": Bernard L. Montgomery, George S. Patton und Erwin Rommell*[853]. ISBN 978-3-643-10349-9.
- Kummer, Silja (1 November 2012). "Feministischer Protest: Rommel-Denkmal mit rosa "Pussy Hat" geschmückt"[854]. Heidenheimer Zeitung. Retrieved 22 August 2017.

- Latimer, Jon (2002). *Alamein*. Cambridge, MA: Harvard University Press. ISBN 978-0-674-01016-1.
- Leithäuser, Johannes (17 August 2017). "Identität und Unbehagen". Frankfurter Allgemeine Zeitung.
- Levine, Alan J. (2007). *D-Day to Berlin: The Northwest Europe Campaign, 1944–45*[855]. Stackpole Books. ISBN 978-1-4617-5085-7.
- Levine, Alan J. (1999). *The War Against Rommel's Supply Lines, 1942-1943*[856]. Praeger. p. 183. ISBN 9780275965211.
- Lewin, Ronald (1998) [1968]. *Rommel As Military Commander*. New York: B&N Books. ISBN 978-0-7607-0861-3.
- Lieb, Peter (2013). "Erwin Rommel. Widerstandskämpfer oder Nationalsozialist?". *Vierteljahrshefte für Zeitgeschichte*. **61**. Degruyter. pp. 303–343.
- Lieb, Peter (2014). "Rommel in Normandy". In I. F. W. Beckett. *Rommel Reconsidered*. Mechanicsburg, PA: Stackpole Books. ISBN 978-0-8117-1462-4.
- Luvaas, Jay (1990). "Liddell Hart and the Mearsheimer Critique: A 'Pupil's' Retrospective"[857] (PDF). *Strategic Studies Institute*. Retrieved 8 February 2016.
- Macksey, Kenneth (1979). *Rommel: Battles and Campaigns*[858]. Arms & Armour Press. ISBN 978-0-85368-232-5.
- Maier, Manfred (2013). "Vortrag Manfred Maier zu der Geschichte des Heidenheimer Rommeldenkmals". In Geschichtswerkstatt Heidenheim. *Vorlage für die Arbeitsgruppe «Umgestaltung des Rommel-Denkmals»*. p. 49.
- Majdalany, Fred (2003). *The Battle of El Alamein: Fortress in the Sand*[859]. University of Pennsylvania Press. pp. 31–32. ISBN 978-0-8122-1850-3.
- Major, Patrick (2008). "'Our Friend Rommel': The Wehrmacht as 'Worthy Enemy' in Postwar British Popular Culture". *German History*. Oxford University Press. **26** (4): 520–535. doi: 10.1093/gerhis/ghn049[860].
- Marshall, Charles F. (1994). *Discovering the Rommel Murder*[861]. Mechanicsburg, Pennsylvania: Stackpole Books. ISBN 978-0-8117-4278-8.
- Mass, Sandra (2006). *Weisse Helden, schwarze Krieger: zur Geschichte kolonialer Männlichkeit in Deutschland 1918–1964*[862]. Böhlau Verlag Köln Weimar. pp. 249, 252, 258, 294, 301. ISBN 978-3-412-32305-9.
- McMahon, T. L. (2014). *Operational Principles: The Operational Art of Erwin Rommel and Bernard Montgomery*[863]. Pickle Partners. ISBN 978-1-78289-742-2.
- Mearsheimer, John (1988). *Liddell Hart and the Weight of History*. Ithaca, N.Y.: Cornell University Press. ISBN 978-0-8014-2089-4.

- Megargee, Geoffrey P. (2000). *Inside Hitler's High Command*. Lawrence, Kansas: Kansas University Press. ISBN 0-7006-1015-4.
- Menne, Evelin. "Warum Umbenennungen sinnvoll sind"[864]. *dielinkelippe.de*. Retrieved 22 August 2017.
- Messenger, Charles (2009). *Rommel: Leadership Lessons from the Desert Fox*. Basingstoke, NY: Palgrave Macmillan. ISBN 0-230-60908-2.
- Mitcham, Samuel W. (1997). *The Desert Fox in Normandy: Rommel's Defense of Fortress Europe*[865]. Greenwood Publishing Group. ISBN 978-0-275-95484-0.
- Mitcham, Jr., Samuel W. (2007a) [1981]. *Rommel's Desert War: The Life and Death of the Afrika Korps*[866]. Stackpole Books. ISBN 978-0-8117-3413-4.
- Mitcham, Jr., Samuel W. (2007b) [1997]. *The Desert Fox in Normandy: Rommel's Defense of Fortress Europe*. Stackpole Books. ISBN 978-0-275-95484-0.
- MDR (12 June 2017). "Wolffsohn: Entscheidung für Rommel-Kaserne richtig"[867]. Mitteldeutsche Rundfunk, ARD. Retrieved 20 August 2017.
- Murray, Williamson (1995). "Knight's Cross, A Life of Field Marshall Erwin Rommel by David Fraser". *The Journal of Military History*. Virginia Military Institute and the George C. Marshall Foundation. **59** (2): 345–346. ISSN 1543-7795[868]. JSTOR 2944594[869].
- Murray, Williamson; Millett, Allan Reed (2009). *A War To Be Won: fighting the Second World War*. Harvard University Press. ISBN 978-0-674-04130-1.
- Murray, Williamson (2011). *Military Adaptation in War: With Fear of Change*[870]. Cambridge University Press. ISBN 978-1-139-91586-1.
- Naumann, Klaus (2009). "Afterword". In Charles Messenger. *Rommel: Leadership Lessons from the Desert Fox*. Basingstoke, NY: Palgrave Macmillan. ISBN 0-230-60908-2.
- Neitzel, Sönke (2005). *Abgehört. Deutsche Generäle in britischer Kriegsgefangenschaft 1942–1945*. Berlin: Propyläen. ISBN 978-3-548-60760-3.
- Paterson, Tony (2011). "Was the Desert Fox an honest soldier or just another Nazi?"[871]. www.independent.co.uk/.
- Pimlott, John, ed. (2014) [1994]. *Rommel: In His Own Words*. London: Amber Books. ISBN 978-1-78274-190-9.
- Pyta, Wolfram (2015). *Hitler: Der Künstler als Politiker und Feldherr. Eine Herrschaftsanalyse*[872]. Siedler Verlag. ISBN 978-3-641-15701-2.
- Remy, Maurice Philip (2002). *Mythos Rommel*. Munich: Ullstein. ISBN 3-548-60385-8. Maurice Philip Remy
- Reuth, Ralf Georg (2005). *Rommel: The End of a Legend*. London: Haus Books. ISBN 978-1-904950-20-2.

- Robinson, James R. (1997). "The Rommel Myth"[873]. *Military Review Journal*. Retrieved 8 February 2016.
- Rommel, Erwin (1982) [1953]. Liddell Hart, B. H., ed. *The Rommel Papers*[874]. New York: Da Capo Press. ISBN 978-0-306-80157-0.
- Rotte, Ralph (3 August 2017). "Richthofen statt Rommel"[875]. FAZ. Frankfurter Allgemeine Zeitung. Retrieved 19 August 2017.
- Sadkovich, James J.; Hixson, Walter L. (2003). *Of Myths and Men: Rommel and the Italians in North Africa, 1940–1942 (chapter) – The American Experience in World War II: The United States in the European theater*[876]. Taylor & Francis. pp. 238–267. ISBN 978-0-415-94033-7.
- C., Schmitt (14 June 2017). "Paderborner Aktionsbündnis übt scharfe Kritik an Namensbeibehaltung der "Rommel-Kaserne""[877]. PaderZeitung. Retrieved 20 August 2017.
- Schnadwinkel, Andreas (10 May 2017). "Rommel-Kaserne will Namen behalten"[878]. WESTFALEN-BLATT. Retrieved 19 August 2017.
- Schrijvers, Peter (1997). *The Crash of Ruin: American Combat Soldiers in Europe during World War II*[879]. Springer. ISBN 9781349145225.
- Searle, Alaric (2014). "Rommel and the rise of the Nazis". In I. F. W. Beckett. *Rommel Reconsidered*. Mechanicsburg, PA: Stackpole Books. ISBN 978-0-8117-1462-4.
- Shirer, William L. (1960). *The Rise and Fall of the Third Reich*. New York: Simon and Schuster. ISBN 978-0-671-62420-0.
- Showalter, Dennis E. (2006). *Patton And Rommel: Men of War in the Twentieth Century* (2006 ed.). New York City, New York: Berkley Books. ISBN 978-0-425-20663-8.
- Smelser, Ronald; Davies, Edward J. (2008). *The Myth of the Eastern Front: The Nazi-Soviet War in American Popular Culture*. New York: Cambridge University Press. ISBN 978-0-521-83365-3. Ronald Smelser
- Stickler, Matthias (2005). "Generalfeldmarschall Erwin Rommel - Ein Mythos im Zwielicht". In Matthias Stickler; Verena Spinnler. *Portraits zur Geschichte des deutschen Widerstands*. Leidorf. p. 189–208. ISBN 9783896468383.
- Stroud, Rick (2013). *The Phantom Army of Alamein: The Men Who Hoodwinked Rommel*[880]. A&C Black. ISBN 978-1-4088-3128-1.
- SWP (4 April 2018). "Bundeswehr Der Name „Rommel" bleibt"[881]. Südwest Presse Online. Retrieved 8 April 2018.
- The Cairns Post (9 September 1941). "Gangster goes to war? Hitler's "white hope""[882]. The Cairns Post. Retrieved 14 September 2017.
- Watson, Bruce Allen (1999). *Exit Rommel: The Tunisian Campaign, 1942–43*[883]. Westport, Conn.: Praeger Publishers. ISBN 978-0-275-95923-4.
- Watson, Bruce Allen (2006). *Exit Rommel: The Tunisian Campaign,*

1942–43[884]. Westport, Conn.: Stackpole Books. ISBN 978-0-8117-3381-6.
- Wette, Wolfram (2007). *The Wehrmacht: History, Myth, Reality*. Cambridge, Mass.: Harvard University Press. ISBN 978-0-674-02577-6.
- Wrobel, Claudia (1 February 2017). "»Das können keine Vorbilder für uns sein«"[885]. Retrieved 18 April 2017.
- Young, Desmond (1950). *Rommel: The Desert Fox*[886]. New York: Harper & Row. OCLC 48067797[887].
- Zabecki, David T. (2016). "Rethinking Rommel"[888]. *Military History*. Herndon, Va. **32** (5): 24–29.
- Zabecki, David T. (2016b). "March 2016 Readers' Letters"[889]. *HistoryNet*. Retrieved 3 March 2016. David T. Zabecki
- Zaloga, Steven (2013). *The Devil's Garden: Rommel's Desperate Defense of Omaha Beach*[890]. Stackpole Books. ISBN 978-0-8117-5277-0.

Further reading

- Lieb, Peter (2012). "Rommel, Field Marshal Erwin (1891–1944)". *The Encyclopedia of War*.

External links

- Myth of 'humane' Nazi Erwin Rommel debunked[891]: 2008 *The Telegraph* news report on "The Rommel Myth" exhibition. Images[892] from the exhibition as they appeared in the book *In Detail, Exhibitions and Displays*.
- "Defeating the Desert Fox": Video[838] on YouTube, via the official channel of The National WWII Museum; session by Nigel Hamilton at the 2012 International Conference on World War II
- " Erwin Rommel: The Hero of the Clean Wehrmacht[893]", via *Die Welt* (in German)

Appendix

References

[1] Remy 2002, p. 15.
[2] Remy 2002, pp. 28, 355, 361.
[3] Scheck 2010.
[4] Butler 2015, pp. 18, 122, 139, 147.
[5] Hart 2014, p. 128-52.
[6] Von Fleischhauer & Friedmann 2012.
[7] Fraser 1993, p. 8.
[8] Butler 2015, pp. 26–27.
[9] Remy 2002, p. 12.
[10] Pimlott 2003, p. 9.
[11] Hoffmann 2004, p. 10.
[12] Butler 2015, pp. 30–31.
[13] Butler 2015, p. 43.
[14] Butler 2015, p. 31.
[15] Lewin 1998, p. 4.
[16] Fraser 1993, pp. 25, 27–29.
[17] Fraser 1993, p. 31.
[18] Fraser 1993, p. 36, 43.
[19] Fraser 1993, pp. 43, 45.
[20] Fraser 1993, p. 19.
[21] Fraser 1993, pp. 53–60.
[22] Butler 2015, pp. 65–67.
[23] Hoffmann 2004, p. 14.
[24] Hoffmann 2004, p. 15.
[25] Butler 2015, pp. 71–77.
[26] Remy 2002, pp. 18–25.
[27] Grossman 1993, pp. 316–335.
[28] House 1985, p. 36.
[29] Carver 2005, p. 321.
[30] Butler 2015, pp. 78–81.
[31] Butler 2015, p. 99.
[32] Butler 2015, p. 100.
[33] Fraser 1993, p. 86.
[34] Reuth 2005, p. 18.
[35] Remy 2015, p. 100.
[36] Fraser 1993, p. 98.
[37] Fraser 1993, p. 100.
[38] Lewin 1998, p. 9.
[39] Fraser 1993, p. 117.
[40] Online version https://www.scribd.com/document/30313896/The-Rommel-Models-Impact-on-Maneuver-Warfare in Scribd.
[41] Butler 2015, pp. 133–134.
[42] Showalter 2006, p. 123.
[43] Remy 2002, pp. 36–37.
[44] Butler 2016, pp. 24–30.
[45] Butler 2015, p. 132.
[46] Fraser 1993, pp. 120–121.
[47] Remy 2002, p. 37.
[48] Searle 2014, pp. 19–21.
[49] Butler 2015, p. 137.

[50] Butler 2015, p. 142.
[51] Butler 2015, pp. 100, 103.
[52] Fraser 1993, p. 99.
[53] Butler 2015, p. 144.
[54] Butler 2015, p. 146.
[55] Fraser 1993, p. 141.
[56] Fraser 1993, p. 146, 149.
[57] Searle 2014, p. 24.
[58] Maier 2013, p. 49.
[59] Butler 2015, p. 151.
[60] Hoffmann 2004, p. 114.
[61] Watson 1999, p. 158.
[62] Caddick-Adams 2012, pp. 125, 141.
[63] Zabecki 2016.
[64] Zaloga 2013, p. 64.
[65] Pimlott 1994, p. 49.
[66] Fraser 1993, pp. 156–157.
[67] Fraser 1993, pp. 151, 161.
[68] Butler 2015, pp. 154–155.
[69] Lewin 1998, p. 14.
[70] Murray & Millett 2009, p. 71.
[71] Butler 2015, pp. 160–161.
[72] Krause & Phillips 2007, p. 176 https://books.google.com/books?id=1DLRMQfzyVwC&pg=PA176..
[73] Butler 2015, p. 164.
[74] Fraser 1993, p. 183.
[75] Butler 2015, pp. 165–166.
[76] Butler 2015, p. 166.
[77] Hoffmann 2004, p. 24.
[78] Krause & Phillips 2007, p. 179.
[79] Messenger 2009, p. 51.
[80] Butler 2015, pp. 169–171.
[81] Butler 2015, pp. 172, 174.
[82] Fraser 1993, pp. 204–206.
[83] Fraser 1993, pp. 191–192.
[84] Butler 2015, p. 177.
[85] Hoffmann 2004, p. 26.
[86] Pimlott 1994, p. 48.
[87] Caddick-Adams 2012, pp. 471–472.
[88] Beckett 2014, Chapter 2 - Claus Telp, "Rommel and 1940", p. 52 https://books.google.com/books?id=Lc07BAAAQBAJ&pg=PA52&dq=rommel+shot+colonel#v=onepage&q=rommel%20shot%20colonel&f=false.
[89] Pimlott 2003, p. 47.
[90] Les crimes nazis lors de la libération de la France (1944–1945) Dominique Lormier 2014.
[91] "Indeed, the soldiers of the 'Ghost Division' and its partner in crime, 5th Panzer Division, committed numerous atrocities against French colonial troops in 1940, murdering fifty surrendered non-commissioned officers and men at Airaines."<ref name="FOOTNOTEAlexander2012332">Alexander 2012, p. 332.
[92] "On 7 June, a number of soldiers of 53eme Regiment d'Infanterie Coloniale were shot, probably by troops of the 5th Panzer Division, following their surrender after a spirited defense in the area of Airaines, near Le Quesnoy. Similar acts had also been perpetrated by soldiers of Rommel's 7th Panzer Division on 5 June against the defenders of Le Quesnoy. Rommel noted in his own account that "any enemy troops were either wiped out or forced to withdraw"; at the same time he also provided the disparaging (but possibly somewhat contradictory in light of his first note) observation that "many of the prisoners taken were hopelessly drunk."<ref name="FOOTNOTEStone2009109">Stone 2009, p. 109.

[93] Les Combats d'Airaines et environs, juin 1940 André Laboulet impr. Lafosse, page 21, 1972.
[94] In Hangest-sur-Somme, some captured Tirailleurs and a French second lieutenant were shot by Germans in black uniforms, most likely members of Rommel's 7th Panzer Division<ref name="FOOTNOTEScheck200626">Scheck 2006, p. 26.
[95] Dominique Lormier: Les crimes nazis lors de la libération de la France (1944–1945)
[96] Butler 2015, p. 173–174.
[97] Patton And Rommel: Men of War in the Twentieth Century - Dennis Showalter - 1996 "In fact, the garrison of Le Quesnoy, most of them Senegalese, took heavy toll of the German infantry in house-to-house fighting. Unlike other occasions in 1940, when Germans and Africans met, there was no deliberate massacre of survivors."
[98] Beckett 2014, p. 52, Chapter 2 - Claus Telp, "Rommel and 1940", https://books.google.com/books?id=Lc07BAAAQBAJ&pg=PA52.
[99] Fraser 1993, p. 223.
[100] Fraser 1993, p. 217.
[101] Butler 2015, p. 17.
[102] Butler 2015, p. 182.
[103] Butler 2015, pp. 187–190.
[104] Remy 2002, p. 56.
[105] Butler 2015, p. 193.
[106] Butler 2015, p. 199.
[107] Butler 2015, p. 198.
[108] Lewin 1998, p. 33.
[109] Fraser 1993, p. 229.
[110] Fraser 1993, p. 231.
[111] Butler 2015, pp. 204–205.
[112] Lewin 1998, p. 36.
[113] Butler 2015, p. 205.
[114] Lewin 1998, p. 35.
[115] Butler 2015, p. 205–206.
[116] Butler 2015, pp. 207, 214.
[117] Fraser 1993, p. 236.
[118] Butler 2015, p. 220.
[119] Butler 2015, p. 221.
[120] Butler 2015, p. 258.
[121] Butler 2015, pp. 221, 224.
[122] Hoffmann 2004, p. 35.
[123] Fraser 1993, p. 242.
[124] Hoffmann 2004, p. 39.
[125] Butler 2015, pp. 240–241.
[126] Butler 2015, p. 244.
[127] Douglas-Home 1973, p. 100.
[128] Butler 2015, p. 250.
[129] Butler 2015, p. 271.
[130] Lewin 1998, p. 48.
[131] Mitcham 2007, pp. 28, 175.
[132] Mitcham 2008, p. 436.
[133] Lewin 1998, p. 53.
[134] Lewin 1998, p. 54.
[135] Lewin 1998, p. 57.
[136] Butler 2015, pp. 292–293.
[137] Butler 2015, p. 293.
[138] Fraser 1993, p. 277.
[139] Fraser 1993, pp. 278–280.
[140] Butler 2015, p. 294.
[141] Butler 2015, p. 295.
[142] Butler 2015, pp. 294–295.

[143] Butler 2015, p. 297.
[144] Butler 2015, p. 298.
[145] Fraser 1993, pp. 287–289.
[146] Butler 2015, pp. 300–301.
[147] Fraser 1993, p. 288.
[148] 23 to 28 November according to Mellenthin.<ref name="FOOTNOTEvon Luck198958">von Luck 1989, p. 58.
[149] Fraser 1993, pp. 291–293.
[150] Butler 2015, p. 304.
[151] Douglas-Home 1973, p. 131.
[152] Lewin 1998, pp. 99–101, Quote from Rommel: I had maintained secrecy over the Panzer Group's forthcoming attack eastwards from Mersa el Brega and informed neither the Italian nor the German High Command. We knew from experience that Italian Headquarters cannot keep things to themselves and that everything they wireless to Rome gets round to British ears. However, I had arranged with the Quartermaster for the Panzer Group's order to be posted in every *Cantoniera* in Tripolitinia on 21 January ....
[153] Butler 2015, pp. 308, 311.
[154] Lewin 1998, p. 106.
[155] Butler 2015, pp. 309–310.
[156] Butler 2015, p. 321.
[157] Butler 2015, p. 319.
[158] Rommel 1982, p. 196.
[159] Butler 2015, pp. 323–324.
[160] Hoffmann 2004, p. 45.
[161] Butler 2015, p. 326.
[162] Butler 2015, pp. 325–327.
[163] Butler 2015, p. 330.
[164] Butler 2015, p. 331.
[165] Rommel 1982, p. 217.
[166] Fraser 1993, p. 334.
[167] Rommel 1982, p. 224.
[168] Butler 2015, pp. 334–335.
[169] Fraser 1993, p. 337.
[170] Butler 2015, p. 337.
[171] As recounted by Luck in his memoirs, Rommel commented to his wife that he wished Hitler had given him another division instead.<ref name="FOOTNOTEvon Luck1989103">von Luck 1989, p. 103.
[172] Playfair 1960, p. 296.
[173] Butler 2015, pp. 285–286, 345–347.
[174] Shirer 1960, pp. 911–912.
[175] Butler 2015, p. 342.
[176] Butler 2015, pp. 339, 343.
[177] Fraser 1993, pp. 343–344.
[178] Butler 2015, pp. 343–344.
[179] Butler 2015, pp. 338–339, 344.
[180] Butler 2015, pp. 347–350.
[181] Shirer 1960, p. 913.
[182] Fraser 1993, p. 345.
[183] Butler 2015, p. 351.
[184] Fraser 1993, p. 346.
[185] Butler 2015, p. 354.
[186] Butler 2015, pp. 355, 370.
[187] Douglas-Home 1973, p. 171.
[188] Douglas-Home 1973, map, p.163.
[189] Hoffmann 2004, pp. 47–48.
[190] Hoffmann 2004, p. 48.

[191] Douglas-Home 1973, p. 165.
[192] Carver 1962, p. 67.
[193] Lewin 1998, p. 160.
[194] Carver 1962, p. 70.
[195] Rommel 1982, p. 286.
[196] Butler 2015, p. 372.
[197] Hoffmann 2004, p. 50.
[198] Hoffmann 2004, p. 52.
[199] Butler 2015, p. 362.
[200] Douglas-Home 1973, p. 172.
[201] Fraser 1993, p. 370.
[202] Rommel 1982, p. 299.
[203] Butler 2015, pp. 375–377.
[204] Fraser 1993, p. 373.
[205] Butler 2015, pp. 378–380.
[206] Fraser 1993, p. 378.
[207] Butler 2015, p. 385.
[208] Fraser 1993, pp. 379–380.
[209] Butler 2015, pp. 385–386.
[210] Butler 2015, pp. 387–388.
[211] Fraser 1993, pp. 381–383.
[212] Rommel 1982, p. 327.
[213] Butler 2015, p. 389.
[214] Fraser 1993, p. 383.
[215] Douglas-Home 1973, p. 179.
[216] Watson 1999, pp. 173–4 https://books.google.com/books?id=Hn9chmb3PSEC&pg=PA174 (2006 ed. Stackpole Books)..
[217] Lewin 1998, p. 190.
[218] Coggins 1980, p. 11.
[219] Lewin 1998, p. 192.
[220] Rommel 1982, pp. 342–357.
[221] Coggins 1980, p. 129.
[222] Coggins 1980, p. 134.
[223] Coggins 1980, p. 135.
[224] Lewin 1998, p. 209.
[225] Coggins 1980, p. 136.
[226] Lieb 2014, p. 115–116.
[227] Lieb 2014, p. 117.
[228] Hoffmann 2004, p. 117.
[229] Willmott 1984, p. 69.
[230] Lewin 1998, p. 213.
[231] Mitcham 1997, p. 15, 23.
[232] Messenger 2009, p. 166.
[233] Brighton 2008, p. 247.
[234] Lieb: Of course, Rommel did not conceive all these devices himself ... His engineer general Wilhelm Meise once called Rommel 'the greatest engineer of the Second World War.<ref name="FOOTNOTELieb2014120">Lieb 2014, p. 120.
[235] Earle Rice, historian and senior design engineer in aerospace and nuclear industries: he would add all manner of ingenious obstacles and impedance devices to the anticipated landing areas. But ... shortages of concrete and other materials and insufficient time prevented him from completing the Atlantic Wall to his satisfaction.<ref name="FOOTNOTERice200989–90">Rice 2009, p. 89–90.
[236] Zaloga, historian and military technology expert: Rommel and his headquarters developed a variety of obstacles to interfere with landing craft. This was Rommel's single most important

contribution to the defense of the Normandy coast ... Rommel's pet project, the coastal obstacles, had proven to be one of the most successful innovations in the German defenses.<ref name="FOOTNOTEZaloga201353, 57">Zaloga 2013, pp. 53, 57.

[237] Ruge: "He did not adhere rigidly to details ... was very open to new ideas and very much interested in technical progress. He grasped the significance of an improvement or an invention very quickly and often added to it. When a new device had been suggested to him during the evening, it was not unusual for Rommel to phone the proposer early the following morning with a proposal of his own which was a definite improvement". Dihm: "Therefore a complete series of instructions were issued. These instructions were partly devised by the Generalfeldmarschall himself and were accompanied by sketches drawn by him. They dealt mainly with the erection of obstacles on the beaches. It was intended to join these barriers to form a continuous line"<ref name="Ruge160415" group="">

[238] Lieb 2014, p. 121.
[239] Rice 2009, p. 90.
[240] Willmott 1984, p. 60.
[241] Caddick-Adams 2013, p. 221.
[242] Mitcham 1997, p. 198.
[243] Willmott 1984, p. 89.
[244] Messenger 2009, p. 168–170.
[245] Willmott 1984, p. 83.
[246] Messenger 2009, p. 169.
[247] Lieb 2014, p. 125.
[248] Hart 2014, p. 146.
[249] Hoffmann 2004, p. 65.
[250] Marshall 1994, p. 137.
[251] Hansen 2014, p. 57.
[252] Beckett 2014, p. 6.
[253] Shirer 1960, pp. 1031, 1177.
[254] Hart 2014, pp. 142–150.
[255] Hart 2014, pp. 139–142.
[256] Hart 2014, pp. 145–146.
[257] Naumann 2009, pp. 189–191.
[258] Remy 2002, pp. 241–355.
[259] Faltin 2014, Cornelia Hecht considered it (Eberbach's testimony) authentic, "Why did he have to lie?".
[260] Hart 2014, p. 140: Sourced to Speidel (1950) *Invasion 1944: We Defended Normandy*, pp. 68, 73.
[261] Hart 2014, pp. 145–147.
[262] Pimlott 2003, pp. 213, 218.
[263] Knopp 2013, p. 81.
[264] Remy 2002, p. 301.
[265] Hansen 2014, p. 46.
[266] Remy 2002, pp. 306.
[267] Remy 2002, pp. 306–307.
[268] Hart 2014, pp. 152.
[269] Hart 2014, pp. 141, 152.
[270] Reuth 2005, p. 183.
[271] Young 1950, p. 197.
[272] Shirer 1960, p. 1031.
[273] Remy 2002, p. 293.
[274] Reuth 2005, p. 198.
[275] Butler 2015, p. 538.
[276] Mitcham 2007, p. 28.
[277] Remy 2002, p. 335.
[278] Reuth 2005, p. 194.
[279] Hansen 2014, p. 70.

[280] Shirer 1960, p. 967.
[281] "Burgdorf had with him copies of the interrogations of von Hofacker, von Stülpnagel and Speidel, along with a letter written by Keitel ostensibly dictated by Hitler himself. In the letter, the Führer gave Rommel an impossible choice: if he believed himself innocent of the allegations against him, then Rommel must report to Hitler in person in Berlin; refusal to do so would be considered an admission of guilt ... There was no mention of Rommel's case first being put to the Wehrmacht's Court of Honor, a curious omission if Rommel were indeed being brought to book as part of von Stauffenberg's conspiracy."<ref name="FOOTNOTEButler2015540–541">Butler 2015, pp. 540–541.
[282] Evans 2009, p. 642.
[283] https://www.telegraph.co.uk/news/worldnews/europe/germany/3836479/Myth-of-humane-Nazi-Erwin-Rommel-debunked.html*Myth of 'humane' Nazi Erwin Rommel debunked* The Telegraph 19 December 2008.
[284] von Fleischhauer & Friedmann 2012.
[285] Butler 2015, p. 540.
[286] Remy 2002, p. 348.
[287] Knopp 2011, p. 416.
[288] Rommel's words, from Maisel's reminiscences: "I will see the consequences. I have forgotten myself."
[289] Remy 2002, pp. 348, 419.
[290] Evans 2009, pp. 642–643.
[291] Manfred Rommel, Nuremberg testimony
[292] "Manfred Rommel, son of the Desert Fox, forged a great friendship with Monty's son which became a symbol of post-war reconciliation" https://www.telegraph.co.uk/news/obituaries/military-obituaries/10439408/Manfred-Rommel.html. *The Daily Telegraph.* 10 November 2013.
[293] "'The Desert Fox' commits suicide" http://www.history.com/this-day-in-history/the-desert-fox-commits-suicide. History. Retrieved 23 August 2014.
[294] Butler 2015, p. 543.
[295] Mitcham 1997, p. 196.
[296] Marshall 1994, p. 169.
[297] Rommel 1982, p. 505, Letter from Goering to Frau Rommel, 26 October 1944: "The fact that your husband, Field Marshal Rommel, has died a hero's death as a result of his wounds, after we had all hoped he would remain for the German people, has deeply touched me.".
[298] Shirer 1960, p. 1078.
[299] Marshall 1994, p. 173.
[300] Manfred Rommel: *Trotz allem heiter.* Stuttgart 1998, 3rd edition, p. 69.
[301] von Mellenthin 1956, p. 321.
[302] Marshall p.
[303] Porch 2004, pp. 205–208.
[304] Lieb 2014, p. 122.
[305] Butler 2015, pp. 241, 281–283.
[306]
[307] Lieb: "Rommel's internal opponents could not hide their satisfaction as the events were unfolding" (Lieb 2014, pp. 122).
[308] Pimlott: His qualities of leadership were high. He cared about his men and was determined from the start of his fighting career to master the tactical skills that would enable them to survive ... it was obvious from the start that Rommel was a cut above the majority of his contemporaries ... The 'Desert Fox' was a genuine hero, revered not just for his personal bravery in battle but also for his apparent ability to outfight a succession of enemy generals, many of whom enjoyed numerical and even technological superiority ... his record ... undoubtedly raised him to the status of a potential saviour of the Fatherland.<ref name="FOOTNOTEPimlott20035, 218">Pimlott 2003, pp. 5, 218.
[309] Ambrose 1994, p. 63.
[310] Rice 2009, p. 38, 42.
[311] Murray & Millett 2009, p. 266.

[312] Butler 2015, pp. 18, 249.
[313] Arquilla 1996, p. 218.
[314] Beckett 2014, Chapter 2 - Claus Telp, "Rommel and 1940", p. 48.
[315] Messenger 2009, p. 2.
[316] Rommel 1982, p. xv, Liddell Hart in the introduction to the Rommel Papers: "Until I delved into Rommel's papers I regarded him as a brilliant tactician and great fighting leader, but did not realize how deep a sense of strategy he had.".
[317] Lieb 2014, pp. 135.
[318] Beckett 2014, Chapter 2 - Claus Telp, "Rommel and 1940", pp. 54.
[319] Lewin 1998, p. 16.
[320] Porch 2004, p. 204.
[321] Butler 2015, p. 168.
[322] Barnett 1989, p. 299.
[323] Hoffmann 2004, p. 101.
[324] Brighton 2008, p. 108.
[325] von Mellenthin 1956, p. 88.
[326] Mitcham 2007, p. 98.
[327] Showalter 2006, p. 210.
[328] Mitcham 2007, p. 102.
[329] Cocks 2012, pp. 206–207.
[330] Lewin 1998, p. 1.
[331] Hoffmann 2004, p. 92.
[332] Lewin 1998, p. 239.
[333] According to Lewin, in 1933 when Rommel became commander of a Hanoverian Jaeger battalion, which was composed of soldiers with skiing expertise, its officers gave him the mandatory test on the snow slopes. No lift was present, and the men had to climb to ski down the hillside. They trudged to the top and descended, and honour was satisfied, but the 41-year-old commander led his officers up and down the slope twice more before he let them fall out.<ref name="FOOTNOTELewin1998239">Lewin 1998, p. 239.
[334] Caddick-Adams 1998, p. 368.
[335] von Mellenthin 1956, p. 45.
[336] Remy 2002, pp. 24, 75, 90.
[337] Watson 1999, pp. 133.
[338] "Diario storico del Comando Supremo", vol.5 to 9, Italian Army General Staff Historical Office
[339] "Verbali delle riunioni tenute dal Capo di SM Generale", vol.2 and 3, Italian Army General Staff Historical Office
[340] Latimer 2002, p. 31.
[341] Montanari, "Le operazioni in Africa Settentrionale", vol. 1 to 4, Italian Army General Staff Historical Office, 1985–1993.
[342] Kesselring, *The Memoirs of Field Marshal Kesselring*, pp. 124–125.
[343] Watson 1999, pp. 164–165.
[344] M.Montanari, Le Operazioni in Africa Settentrionale, Vol.IV, chapter III, 1985–1993, pp. 119–197.
[345] Spiegel quoted Goebbels: "Rommel is amazingly popular with the troops, German and Italian. He is almost a mythical figure."<ref name="FOOTNOTEVon FleischhauerFriedmann2012">Von Fleischhauer & Friedmann 2012.
[346] Butler 2015, p. 352–353.
[347] Marshall 1994, p. 93.
[348] Lieb 2014, p. 115.
[349] Coggins 1980, p. 30.
[350] Lewin 1998, pp. 241–242.
[351] Beckett 2013, p. 52.
[352] Young 1950, pp. 127–128.
[353] von Luck 1989, pp. 125–128.
[354] Lieb 2013, pp. 26–27.
[355] Remy 2002, pp. 203–205.

[356] Lieb 2014, pp. 129–130.
[357] Lieb 2014, p. 130.
[358] Zbrodnie Wehrmachtu na jeńcach wojennych armii regularnych w II wojnie światowej Szymon Datner Wydawn. Ministerstwa Obrony Narodowej, 1964, page 254.
[359] Beckett 2014, Chapter 2 - Claus Telp, "Rommel and 1940", https://books.google.com/books?id=Lc07BAAAQBAJ&pg=PA52.
[360] Remy 2002, pp. 245, 361.
[361] Remy 2002, p. 44.
[362] Butler 2015, p. 148 https://books.google.com/books?id=u4L3CQAAQBAJ&pg=PA148&dq=rommel+polish+priest&hl=en&redir_esc=y..
[363] Searle 2014, p. 25–6 https://books.google.com/books?id=h8Y7BAAAQBAJ&pg=PA26&redir_esc=y#v=onepage&q&f=false.
[364] Lieb 2014, p. 129.
[365] Evans 2009, pp. 150–151.
[366] Benishay 2016.
[367] Cohen 2015.
[368] Shepherd 2016, p. 357.
[369] Kitchen 2009, p. 10.
[370] Remy 2002, p. 96.
[371] Marshall 1994, p. 258.
[372] Perry 2012, p. 165.
[373] Mitcham's Life and Death of the Afrika Korps: "OKW sent an order ... spoke of numerous German "political refugees" (that is, Jews) ...
[374] Lewin 1998, p. 225.
[375] Jeanne Manning, Jeanne (1999). *A Time to Speak* https://books.google.com/books?id=tR63XIlcC7wC&pg=PA377&dq=Todt+Organization+Rommel+normandy&hl=en&redir_esc=y. Turner Publishing Company. p. 377. ISBN 978-1-56311-560-8.
Rice 2009, p. 88.
[376] Marshall 1994, p. 121.
[377] Holderfield & Varhola 2009, p. 36 https://books.google.com/books?id=xJs6WStOP2oC&pg=PA36..
[378] Lepage, Jean-Denis G.G. (20 October 2015). *Hitler's Armed Forces Auxiliaries: An Illustrated History of the Wehrmachtsgefolge, 1933–1945* https://books.google.com/books?id=AMv-CgAAQBAJ&pg=PA36&dq=atlantic+wall+todt+slave&hl=en&redir_esc=y. McFarland. p. 36. ISBN 978-0-7864-9745-4.
Holderfield & Varhola 2009, p. 34.
[379] Beevor 2009, p. 37.
[380] Colin 2012, p. 76.
[381] Atkinson 2013, p. 83.
[382] Remy 2002, p. 304.
[383] Hecht (editor) 2008, p. 97.
[384] Butler 2015, p. 474.
[385] Latimer 2002, pp. 27.
[386] Remy:"On 8 August 1914, ... Rommel discovered that he had unusual charisma ... This effect (he had on the troops) would become the fundamental element of Mythos Rommel.",<ref name="FOOTNOTERemy200216">Remy 2002, p. 16.
[387] Der Spiegel: "The Wehrmacht had many capable generals ... but none had the charisma of the Swabian with that distinctive round head.",<ref name="FOOTNOTEVon FleischhauerFriedmann2012">Von Fleischhauer & Friedmann 2012.
[388] Messenger 2009, p. 179.
[389] Majdalany: Rommel was, among other things, clever at public relations.<ref name="FOOTNOTEMajdalany200331">Majdalany 2003, p. 31.
[390] Hansen 2014, p. 46–47.
[391] Watson 1999, pp. 158–159.

³⁹²Niall Barr: "... came to fame in a theatre which held almost no strategic interest for Hitler whatsoever".(Barr 2014, p. 60). Martin Kitchen: "German historians have largely ignored the North African campaign, not only because it was peripheral ...".(Kitchen 2009, p. 9).
³⁹³Caddick-Adams 2012, pp. 210–211.
³⁹⁴Watson 1999, p. 159.
³⁹⁵Reuth 2005, p. 124.
³⁹⁶Citino 2012.
³⁹⁷Reuth 2005, pp. 136–139.
³⁹⁸Caddick-Adams 2012, p. 471.
³⁹⁹Peter Caddick-Adams: "Rommel's advances over the winter 1941–42 became a very useful distraction away from Germany's failure before Moscow".<ref name="FOOTNOTECaddick-Adams2012471">Caddick-Adams 2012, p. 471.
⁴⁰⁰Watson 1999, pp. 166–167.
⁴⁰¹Reuth 2005, pp. 141–143.
⁴⁰²Reuth 2005, p. 144.
⁴⁰³Quote from one of Rommel's letters, January 1942: "The opinion of me in the world press has improved".<ref name="FOOTNOTEReuth2005144">Reuth 2005, p. 144.
⁴⁰⁴Zaloga 2013, p. 24.
⁴⁰⁵Reuth 2005, p. 148.
⁴⁰⁶Reuth 2005, pp. 144–146.
⁴⁰⁷Reuth 2005, pp. 150–152.
⁴⁰⁸Reuth 2005, pp. 154–158.
⁴⁰⁹Peter Lieb: "Hitler was well aware that it would be unwise (...) to link the downfall of Army Group Africa to the name of Rommel, the child of Joseph Goebbel's propaganda machinery".<ref name="FOOTNOTELieb2014113">Lieb 2014, p. 113.
⁴¹⁰Lieb 2014, pp. 113–115, 117–118.
⁴¹¹Lieb 2014, pp. 117–118.
⁴¹²Lieb 2014, p. 120.
⁴¹³Reuth 2005, p. 159.
⁴¹⁴Reuth 2005, pp. 159–161.
⁴¹⁵Remy 2002, p. 247.
⁴¹⁶Rommel 1982, p. 241.
⁴¹⁷Rommel 1982, p. 324.
⁴¹⁸Watson 1999, pp. 138, 139.
⁴¹⁹Butler 2015, p. 336.
⁴²⁰Watson 1999, p. 137.
⁴²¹Butler 2015, p. 138.
⁴²²Naumann 2009, p. 190.
⁴²³Reuth 2005, p. 54.
⁴²⁴Messenger 2009, pp. 185–186.
⁴²⁵Robert Citino: "His career had been based solely on Hitler's favor, and we might reasonably describe his attitude toward the Führer as worshipful."<ref name="FOOTNOTECitino2012">Citino 2012.
⁴²⁶Caddick-Adams 2012, p. 472.
⁴²⁷Remy 2002, p. 282.
⁴²⁸Remy 2002, p. 41.
⁴²⁹Messenger 2009, p. 60.
⁴³⁰Charles Messenger: "He [Rommel] did receive one present that pleased him. He had sent Hitler a meticulously prepared diary of his division's exploits and received a letter of thanks just before Christmas. 'You can be proud of your achievements', Hitler wrote."<ref name="FOOTNOTEMessenger200960">Messenger 2009, p. 60.
⁴³¹Inside The Third Reich by Albert Speer, 2015, Hachette UK, - "He was bitterly annoyed with Rommel, who would often give extremely unclear bulletins on the day's movements. In other words, he "veiled" them from headquarters, sometimes for days, only to report an entirely changed situation. Hitler liked Rommel personally but could ill brook this sort of conduct."
⁴³²Remy 2002, p. 355.

[433] Remy 2002, p. 253.
[434] Remy 2002, pp. 281, 282.
[435] Blumentritt 1952, pp. 203.
[436] Remy 2002, pp. 188, 348.
[437] Watson 1999, pp. 170.
[438] Klaus Naumann: "Rommel was used by the Nazi regime to create a myth. He tolerated this since he had a strong dose of personal ambition and vanity."<ref name="FOOTNOTENaumann2009190">Naumann 2009, p. 190.
[439] Maurice Remy: "... Rommel wollte bleiben, was es war: ein Mann der Truppe."<ref name="FOOTNOTERemy200224-25">Remy 2002, pp. 24–25.
[440] Remy 2002, p. 24.
[441] Pyta 2015, p. 605.
[442] Watson 1999, p. 169.
[443] "Patton And Rommel: Men of War in the Twentieth Century" - Dennis Showalter - 2006 "This, he declared, was war as Frederick the Great's cavalry generals had waged it. Seydlitz and Ziethen had led from the front and exploited fleeting opportunities to win tactical victories. Modern generals must do the same thing at the operational level, with tanks replacing horses."
[444] Brighton 2008, p. 5.
[445] Caddick-Adams 2012, p. 427.
[446] Mitcham 2014, p. 6.
[447] Remy 2002, p. 42.
[448] Butler 2015, p. 112.
[449] Remy 2002, p. 327.
[450] Marshall 1994, p. 199.
[451] Butler 2015, p. 516.
[452] Butler 2015, p. 240.
[453] Kubetzky: "Politics-wise, he has nothing but fantastic conceptions." (Goebbels' diary, after the assassination)<ref name="FOOTNOTEKubetzky2010250">Kubetzky 2010, p. 250.
[454] Pyta 2015, pp. 502–521.
[455] Remy 2002, p. 38.
[456] Remy 2002, p. 336.
[457] Reuth 2005, p. 186.
[458] Watson 1999, p. 175.
[459] Erwin Rommel: "During the whole of this period my bitterest enemy was Goering. I think he wanted to get me sacked in order to realise his own plans in North Africa."<ref name="FOOTNOTERommel1982367">Rommel 1982, p. 367.
[460] Butler 2015, p. 283.
[461] Erwin Rommel: "I was not very happy at the prospect of having to go on playing whipping-boy for the Fuehrer s H.Q, the Commando Supremo and the Luftwaffe."<ref name="FOOTNOTERommel1982196">Rommel 1982, p. 196.
[462] Butler 2015, p. 535.
[463] Remy 2002, pp. 38, 361.
[464] Caddick-Adams 2012, pp. 471–473.
[465] Remy 2002, p. 9, 12.
[466] "The masks he wore reflected the genuine plurality of the man"<ref name="FOOTNOTEWatson2006181">Watson 2006, p. 181.
[467] Showalter 2006, p. 7.
[468] Watson 1999, pp. 157–158.
[469] Major 2008.
[470] Ball 2016, pp. 92,102–104.
[471] Searle 2014, p. 9.
[472] Churchill 1950, p. 200.
[473] Searle 2014, pp. 8, 27.
[474] Caddick-Adams 2012, p. 478.
[475] Beckett 2014, I.F.W. Beckett, Introduction, pp. 1–2.

[476] Martin Kitchen: "Early biographies, such as that by Desmond Young, were positively adulatory."(Kitchen 2009, p. 9).
[477] Major 2008, p. 522.
[478] Patrick Major: "Young had relied extensively on interviews with the Field Marshal's surviving widow, son and former comrades so that the positive picture that emerged is perhaps hardly surprising. Yet the overall effect bordered on hagiography".<ref name="FOOTNOTEMajor2008522">Major 2008, p. 522.
[479] Major 2008, p. 521.
[480] Caddick-Adams 2012, p. 474.
[481] Connelly 2014, p. 163.
[482] Major 2008, p. 526.
[483] Mearsheimer 1988, pp. 199–200.
[484] Luvaas 1990, pp. 12–13.
[485] Caddick-Adams 2012, p. 483.
[486] Kitchen: "The North African campaign has usually been seen, as in the title of Rommel's account, as 'War without Hate', and thus as further proof that the German army was not involved in any sordid butchering, which was left to Himmler's SS. While it was perfectly true that the German troops in North Africa fought with great distinction and gallantry, (...) it was fortunate for their subsequent reputation that the SS murderers that followed in their wake did not have an opportunity to get to work."<ref name="FOOTNOTEKitchen200910">Kitchen 2009, p. 10.
[487] Watson 1999, pp. 157–161.
[488] Friedmann 2007.
[489] Spiegel Online: "Gentleman warrior, military genius. The legend of Erwin Rommel, the German Field Marshal who outfoxed the British in North Africa, lives on."<ref name="FOOTNOTEFriedmann2007">Friedmann 2007.
[490] Knopp 2013, p. 54.
[491] Strawson 2014, p. 124.
[492] Wistrich 2001, p. 107.
[493] Holmes 2009, p. 129.
[494] Bradford 2011, pp. 66, 183.
[495] Sadler 2016, p. 63.
[496] Butler 2015, pp. 410, 551.
[497] Beckett 2014, I.F.W. Beckett, Introduction, pp. 4–6.
[498] Caddick-Adams 2012, pp. 485–486.
[499] Watson 1999, p. 122.
[500] Hansen 2014, pp. 48, 69, 71, 354.
[501] Remy 2002, p. 10.
[502] Terry Brighton. *Patton, Montgomery, Rommel: Masters of War*. New York: Crown, 2008. p. xvii.
[503] According to David T. Zabecki, Rommel's insubordination also played a role, leading to a calamitous misuse of resources when Rommel went over the head of his superior, Field Marshal Albert Kesselring, to appeal directly to Hitler to approve an assault on Egypt instead of occupying Malta, as Kesselring and OKW were planning.<ref name="FOOTNOTEZabecki2016">Zabecki 2016.
[504] Naumann 2009, pp. 189–190.
[505] Klaus Naumann: "Rommel's way out in Africa—bypassing the chain of command by seeking direct access to Hitler—must never be taken as an example to be followed." This allowed him to achieve some tactical victories, but this contributed to eventual operational and strategic failure in North Africa.<ref name="FOOTNOTENaumann2009189–190">Naumann 2009, pp. 189–190.
[506] Watson 1999, p. 118.
[507] Däniker 2002, p. 117.
[508] vom Hagen 2014, pp. 183–184.
[509] Robert Citino: "[Rommel's] disinterest in the dreary science of logistics, his love of action, his tendency to fly off to wherever the fighting was hottest—all of these qualities (...) are problems in a commander under modern conditions, and they all contributed materially to the disaster that

ultimately befell him and his army in the desert."<ref name="FOOTNOTECitino2012">Citino 2012.
[510] Addington 1967.
[511] Porch 2004, p. 206.
[512] Megargee 2000, p. 97.
[513] Zabecki March 2016.
[514] Lieb 2014.
[515] Remy: Kesselring, ... in his memoirs that criticizes the five year younger and much more popular Rommel, ... he already knew at least since the war's end about American arms shipment and intention to intervene which would rendered the strategical value of Malta meaningless, that left Rommel only one choice ...<ref name="FOOTNORemy2002107">Remy 2002, p. 107.
[516] Mitcham: General Warlimont of the High Command later wrote that he "could in any case hardly have acted differently" in ordering the pursuit.General Warlimont and Rommel were not exactly the best of friends ... If this man, a member of OKW in Berlin, endorsed Rommel's decision after the fact, then the logic behind the decision must have been compelling. With American industrial production beginning to make itself felt, while Germany bled herself white on the Russian Front, any chance of scoring a decisive victory had to be taken<ref name="FOOTNOTEMitcham2007139">Mitcham 2007, p. 139.
[517] Mitcham 2009, p. 154.
[518] Moorhouse 2007, pp. 157–158.
[519] Butler 2015, p. 32.
[520] Butler 2015, pp. 32–33.
[521] Butler 2015, p. 101.
[522] Butler 2015, pp. 33, 104.
[523] Butler 2015, p. 546.
[524] Finklestone 2013, p. 16.
[525] Butler 2015, photos after p. 240.
[526] Fraser 1993, p. 43.
[527] Butler 2015, p. 561.
[528] Fraser 1993, p. 172.
[529] Scherzer 2007, p. 638.
[530] Butler 2015, p. 315.
[531] Uwe Walter, *Die Strukturen und Verbände des deutschen Heeres*, vol. 1, 2017
[532] Wolfgang Harnack: *Die Zerstörerflottille der Deutschen Marine von 1958 bis heute*. Koehlers Verlagsgesellschaft, Hamburg 2001,
[533] *Museen in Baden-Württemberg*, Landesstelle für Museumsbetreuung Baden-Württemberg and Museumsverband Baden-Württemberg 2013, 7th ed., Konrad Theiss Verlag Stuttgart, p. 70
[534] Michael Haag, *Egypt*, p. 394, New Holland, 2004,
[535] http://search.proquest.com/openview/b33d63e4fad97fd0ada138379cca9549/1?pq-origsite=gscholar&cbl=1819215
[536] https://books.google.com/books?id=0NzeDAAAQBAJ
[537] http://www.lphinfo.com/le-journal-de-bord-du-chef-ss-en-tunisie-decouvert/
[538] https://books.google.com/books?id=Jcc-AAAAYAAJ&q=%22Standing+by+Rommel,+it+could+be+observed+with+what+animation+Hitler+and+he+conversed+together%22
[539] https://books.google.com/books?id=SyTOAwAAQBAJ&pg=PA97
[540] https://books.google.com/books/about/Field_Marshal.html?id=u4L3CQAAQBAJ
[541] https://archive.org/details/SSHitlerjugendTheHistoryOfTheTwelfthSSDivision194345
[542] https://books.google.com/books?id=ZijAAwAAQBAJ&pg=PT321
[543] //www.worldcat.org/oclc/396145
[544] //www.worldcat.org/oclc/396147
[545] http://www.historynet.com/rommels-afrika-korps.htm
[546] http://www.ynetnews.com/articles/0,7340,L-4647858,00.html
[547] http//www.stuttgarter-zeitung.de
[548] https://books.google.com/books?id=jVD5AQAAQBAJ&pg=PA16
[549] http://www.spiegel.de/spiegel/print/d-89343538.html

[550] http://www.spiegel.de/international/germany/world-war-ii-new-research-taints-image-of-desert-fox-rommel-a-484510.html
[551] https://books.google.com/books?id=H_ginDMhCsMC&pg=PA129
[552] https://books.google.com/books?id=AUZdQaUesoMC&pg=PA36
[553] http://strategicstudiesinstitute.army.mil/pubs/parameters/articles/1990/1990%20luvaas.pdf
[554] //doi.org/10.1093/gerhis/ghn049
[555] https://books.google.com/books?id=HBQ3Va075OoC&pg=PA198
[556] https://books.google.com/books?id=VckKAAAAQBAJ
[557] https://books.google.com/books?redir_esc=y&id=e6UiAQAAIAAJ
[558] https://archive.org/details/THEROMMELPAPERS
[559] https://books.google.com/books?id=1WMdDAAAQBAJ&pg=PT63
[560] http://www.perspectivia.net/publikationen/francia/francia-recensio/2010-3/ZG/mythos-rommel_scheck
[561] https://books.google.com/books?id=bE1E2My2jvoC
[562] https://books.google.com/books?id=hdYTAAAAQBAJ&pg=PA124
[563] http://www.abc-clio.com/Praeger/product.aspx?pc=C7101C
[564] https://archive.org/stream/RommelDesmondYoung/Rommel%20-%20Desmond%20Young_djvu.txt
[565] //www.worldcat.org/oclc/48067797
[566] http://www.historynet.com/military-history-january-2016-table-of-contents-2.htm
[567] http://www.historynet.com/march-2016-readers-letters.htm
[568] https://www.reuters.com/article/entertainment-us-germany-rommel-idUSBRE8A00RM20121101
[569] https://kuecprd.ku.edu/~upress/cgi-bin/978-0-7006-1791-3.html
[570] http://www.dtic.mil/dtic/tr/fulltext/u2/a393741.pdf
[571] https://books.google.com/books?id=iFDgBQAAQBAJ&pg=PT502
[572] https://www.questia.com/library/journal/1P3-26324710/the-rommel-myth
[573] https://archive.org
[574] http://www.biography.com/people/erwin-rommel-39971
[575] https://daten.digitale-sammlungen.de/0001/bsb00016410/images/index.html?seite=37
[576] https://www.deutsche-biographie.de/ppn118602446.html
[577] //worldcat.org/identities/lccn-n78-95764
[578] https://www.youtube.com/watch?v=VURvlMfdTgg
[579] https://www.dhm.de/lemo/biografie/biografie-erwin-rommel.html
[580] http://purl.org/pressemappe20/folder/pe/014928
[581] Young 1950, p. 26.
[582] Rommel & Liddell Hart 1953, p. xv.
[583] Major 2008, p. 523.
[584] Beckett 2014, pp. 1–2.
[585] Pyta 2015, p. 502.
[586] Echternkamp 2010, p. 114.
[587] Knopp 2013.
[588] Mass 2006, p. 254.
[589] Watson 1999, pp. 157–158.
[590] Caddick-Adams 2012, pp. 471–472.
[591] Beevor 2012, pp. 89–90.
[592] Caddick-Adams 2012, pp. 210–211.
[593] Watson 1999, pp. 158–159.
[594] Niall Barr: "... came to fame in a theatre which held almost no strategic interest for Hitler whatsoever."<ref name="FOOTNOTEBarr201460">Barr 2014, p. 60.
[595] Kitchen 2009, p. 9.
[596] Robinson 1997.
[597] Watson 1999, p. 159.
[598] Reuth 2005, p. 124.
[599] Citino 2012.
[600] Kubetzky 2010, p. 316.

[601] The Cairns Post 1941.
[602] Reuth 2005, pp. 136–139.
[603] Caddick-Adams 2012, p. 471.
[604] Peter Caddick-Adams: "Rommel's advances over the winter 1941–42 became a very useful distraction away from Germany's failure before Moscow."<ref name="FOOTNOTECaddick-Adams2012471">Caddick-Adams 2012, p. 471.
[605] Watson 1999, pp. 166–167.
[606] Reuth 2005, pp. 141–143.
[607] Schrijvers 1997, pp. 63–64.
[608] Deuel 1943, p. 72.
[609] Goldschmidt Waldeck 1943, p. 25.
[610] Holles 1945, p. 227.
[611] Reuth 2005, p. 144.
[612] Quote from one of Rommel's letters, January 1942: "The opinion of me in the world press has improved."<ref name="FOOTNOTEReuth2005144">Reuth 2005, p. 144.
[613] Reuth 2005, p. 148.
[614] Reuth 2005, pp. 144–146.
[615] Reuth 2005, pp. 150–152.
[616] Reuth 2005, pp. 154–158.
[617] Peter Lieb: "Hitler was well aware that it would be unwise ... to link the downfall of Army Group Africa to the name of Rommel, the child of Joseph Goebbel's propaganda machinery."<ref name="FOOTNOTELieb2014113">Lieb 2014, p. 113.
[618] Lieb 2014, pp. 113–115.
[619] Lieb 2014, pp. 117–118.
[620] Lieb 2014, p. 120.
[621] Reuth 2005, p. 159.
[622] Reuth 2005, pp. 159–161.
[623] Ceva 1990, pp. 97–98.
[624] Caddick-Adams 2012, pp. 471–473.
[625] Searle 2014, p. 9.
[626] Smelser & Davies 2008, pp. 72–73.
[627] Wette 2007, pp. 236–237.
[628] Reuth 2005, p. 2.
[629] Searle 2014, pp. 8, 27.
[630] Caddick-Adams 2012, p. 478.
[631] Martin Kitchen: "Early biographies, such as that by Desmond Young, were positively adulatory."<ref name="FOOTNOTEKitchen20099">Kitchen 2009, p. 9.
[632] Major 2008, p. 522.
[633] Patrick Major: "Young had relied extensively on interviews with the Field Marshal's surviving widow, son and former comrades so that the positive picture that emerged is perhaps hardly surprising. Yet the overall effect bordered on hagiography."<ref name="FOOTNOTEMajor2008522">Major 2008, p. 522.
[634] Major 2008, p. 521.
[635] Caddick-Adams 2012, p. 474.
[636] Time 1951.
[637] Major 2008, p. 524.
[638] Major 2008, pp. 524–525.
[639] Caddick-Adams 2012, pp. 480–481.
[640] Chambers 2012.
[641] Caddick-Adams 2012, p. 481.
[642] Major 2008, p. 525.
[643] Major writes, quoting Liddell Hart: "'went to see it in a very critical frame of mind, from past experience of "Hollywood" handling of history', but 'was pleasantly surprised'".<ref name="FOOTNOTEMajor2008525">Major 2008, p. 525.
[644]
[645]

[646] Major 2008, p. 526.
[647] Mearsheimer 1988, pp. 199–200.
[648] Luvaas 1990, pp. 12–13.
[649] Fraser 1993.
[650] Searle 2014, pp. 7, 26.
[651] Major 2008, p. 527.
[652] Hachten Wee & Wee 2004, p. 61.
[653] Murray 2011, p. 146.
[654] Murray 1995, p. 345.
[655] Battistelli 2012, p. 63.
[656] Connelly 2014, p. 169.
[657] Connelly 2014, pp. 162–163.
[658] Watson 1999, pp. 157–161.
[659]
[660] Caddick-Adams 2012, p. 483.
[661] Kitchen: "The North African campaign has usually been seen, as in the title of Rommel's account, as 'War without Hate', and thus as further proof that the German army was not involved in any sordid butchering, which was left to Himmler's SS. While it was perfectly true that the German troops in North Africa fought with great distinction and gallantry, ... it was fortunate for their subsequent reputation that the SS murderers that followed in their wake did not have an opportunity to get to work." Kitchen further explains that the sparsely populated desert areas did not lend themselves to ethnic cleansing; that the German forces never reached Egypt and Palestine, which had large Jewish populations; and that, in the urban areas of Tunisia and Tripolitania, the Italian government constrained the German efforts to discriminate against or eliminate Jews who were Italian citizens.<ref name="FOOTNOTEKitchen200910">Kitchen 2009, p. 10.
[662] Friedmann 2007.
[663] *Spiegel Online*: "Gentleman warrior, military genius. The legend of Erwin Rommel, the German Field Marshal who outfoxed the British in North Africa, lives on."<ref name="FOOTNOTEFriedmann2007">Friedmann 2007.
[664] Waldeck 1943, pp. 24–26.
[665] Mass 2006, pp. 249, 252, 258, 294, 301.
[666] Duffy & Ricci 2013, p. 186.
[667] Calder 2012, pp. 242, 265, 304, 524, 564.
[668] Lewin 1998, p. 9.
[669] Butler 2015, p. 138.
[670] Naumann 2009, p. 190.
[671] Watson 1999, p. 158.
[672] Remy 2002, pp. 30–35.
[673] Butler 2015, p. 122.
[674] Zabecki 2016.
[675] Reuth 2005, p. 54.
[676] Messenger 2009, pp. 185–186.
[677] Robert Citino: "His career had been based solely on Hitler's favor, and we might reasonably describe his attitude toward the Führer as worshipful."<ref name="FOOTNOTECitino2012">Citino 2012.
[678] Caddick-Adams 2012, p. 472.
[679] Hamilton 2012.
[680] Remy 2002, p. 39.
[681] Searle 2014, pp. 19–21.
[682] Remy 2002, pp. 368, 436.
[683] Searle 2014, p. 24.
[684] Maier 2013, p. 49.
[685] Showalter 2006, p. 128.
[686] Messenger 2009, p. 60.
[687] Remy 2012, p. 51.

[688] Atkinson 2013, p. 83.
[689] Atkinson 2002, p. 320.
[690] Reuth 2005, p. 83.
[691] Caddick-Adams 2012, p. 142.
[692] Ball 2016, p. 92.
[693] Baxter 2014, pp. 28–29.
[694] Creveld 1977, pp. 195–201.
[695] Beckett 2014, pp. 4–6.
[696] Robert Citino: "His disinterest in the dreary science of logistics, his love of action, his tendency to fly off to wherever the fighting was hottest—all of these qualities ... are problems in a commander under modern conditions, and they all contributed materially to the disaster that ultimately befell him and his army in the desert."<ref name="FOOTNOTECitino2012">Citino 2012.
[697] Addington 1967.
[698] Megargee 2000, p. 97.
[699] Watson 1999, pp. 164–165.
[700] According to David T. Zabecki, Rommel's insubordination also played a role, leading to a calamitous misuse of resources when Rommel went over the head of his superior, Field Marshal Albert Kesselring, to appeal directly to Hitler to approve an assault on Egypt instead of occupying Malta, as Kesselring and OKW were planning.<ref name="FOOTNOTEZabecki2016">Zabecki 2016.
[701] Naumann 2009, pp. 189–190.
[702] Klaus Naumann: "Rommel's way out in Africa—bypassing the chain of command by seeking direct access to Hitler—must never be taken as an example to be followed." Naumann states that, as "one of the battle-proven principles", "unity of command must be preserved". Rommel did not follow this principle, which allowed him to achieve some tactical victories, but this contributed to eventual operational and strategic failure in North Africa. <ref name="FOOTNOTENaumann2009189-190">Naumann 2009, pp. 189–190.
[703] Zabecki March 2016.
[704] Lieb 2014.
[705] Hanley 2008, p. 180.
[706] Mitcham 2007a, pp. 9, 161.
[707] Mitcham 2007b, p. 233.
[708] Butler 2015, pp. 281, 346, 383, 405, 550, 552.
[709] Krause & Phillips 2006, pp. 175–179.
[710] Stroud 2013, pp. 33–34.
[711] Levine 2007, pp. 14–15.
[712] Knox 2000, pp. 2, 3, 10, 29, 116, 118.
[713] Knorr 2015, p. 79.
[714] Atkinson 2002, pp. 318–319.
[715] Lewin 1998, p. 26.
[716] Boog 2001, p. 839.
[717] Austin 2004, p. 20.
[718] Levine 1999, p. 184.
[719] Hartmann 2011, p. 138.
[720] Butler 2015, p. 259.
[721] Mitcham 2007a, p. 124.
[722] Beckett 2014, p. 6.
[723] Shirer 1960, pp. 1031, 1177.
[724] Hart 2014, pp. 142–150.
[725] Hart 2014, pp. 139–142.
[726] Hart 2014, p. 146.
[727] Hart 2014, pp. 145–146.
[728] Hart 2014, p. 140: Sourced to Speidel (1950) *Invasion 1944: We Defended Normandy*, pp. 68, 73.
[729] Reuth 2005, p. tbd.

[730] Evans 2009, p. 642.
[731] Hart 2014, p. 152.
[732] Blumenson 2001, p. 375.
[733] Brighton 2008, p. 160.
[734] Butler 2015, p. 528.
[735] Hart 2014, pp. 141, 152.
[736] Reuth 2005, p. 183.
[737] Remy 2002, p. 277.
[738] Neitzel 2005, p. 137.
[739] Lieb 2013, p. 343.
[740] Watson 1999, p. 169.
[741] Coetzee 2013, p. 286.
[742] Remy 2002, pp. 24, 75, 90.
[743] Barnett 1989, p. 293.
[744] Brighton 2009, p. 250.
[745] Hansen 2014, pp. 46–47.
[746] Connelly 2009, p. 107.
[747] Klaus Naumann: "Rommel was used by the Nazi regime to create a myth. He tolerated this since he had a strong dose of personal ambition and vanity."<ref name="FOOTNOTENaumann2009190">Naumann 2009, p. 190.
[748] Remy 2002, p. 336.
[749] Dixon 2016, p. 381.
[750] Remy 2002, p. 90.
[751] Hansen 2014, p. 48.
[752] Fischer 2014.
[753] Detsch 2002.
[754] Pyta 2015, pp. 498,502,503.
[755] Watson 1999, pp. 162–163.
[756] Pimlott 2014, pp. 8, 106, 220.
[757] Murray 2009, pp. 100—101.
[758] Major 2008, p. 534.
[759] Reuth 2005, p. 222.
[760] Mitcham, Jr. 1997, pp. 35–36.
[761] Dowe & Hecht 2016, pp. 129–160.
[762] Gabel 2014, p. 202.
[763] Stickler 2005, pp. 189–208.
[764] Watson 2006, p. 181.
[765] Edwards 2012, p. 181.
[766] Battistelli: "The myth of Erwin Rommel – the 'Desert Fox' – has proved to be particularly long lasting. There are many historical issues surrounding his true merits as a military commander and the extent of his actual involvement in the anti-Hitler conspiracy, and yet on close inspection he comes across as a simple, straightforward man whose talents and character ensured his success in the very particular circumstances that arose throughout his career."<ref name="FOOTNOTEBattistelli20124">Battistelli 2012, p. 4.
[767] Hansen 2014, pp. 46–48.
[768] Baxter 2014, p. 58.
[769] McMahon 2014, p. 97.
[770] Brighton 2009, p. 390.
[771] Mitcham, Jr. 2007a, p. 15.
[772] Marshall 1994, p. 169.
[773] Majdalany 2003, p. 32.
[774] Latimer 2002, pp. 27.
[775] Showalter 2006, p. 200.
[776] Giordano: "Another brick is broken out of the mendacious myth of the legendary "Desert Fox" and alleged resistance fighter against Hitler, Field Marshal Erwin Rommel ..."<ref name="FOOTNOTEGiordano2010286">Giordano 2010, p. 286.

[777] Giordano 2000, p. 314–394, 423.
[778] Sadkovich 2003, pp. 238–267.
[779] Kitchen 2014, p. 84.
[780] Citino 2007, p. 117.
[781] Macksey 1979, p. 216.
[782] Schnadwinkel 2017.
[783] Knab 2017.
[784] Rotte 2017.
[785] Schmitt 2017.
[786] Heiducoff 2017.
[787] Kummer 2017.
[788] Menne 2017.
[789] Kanold 2017.
[790] Böhmer 2012.
[791] MDR 2017.
[792] Hagen 2014, pp. 183–184.
[793] Knab 1999, pp. 16–17.
[794] Hecht 2008, p. 128.
[795] Leithäuser 2017.
[796] SWP 2018.
[797] Bartels 2017.
[798] FAZ 2018.
[799] Wrobel 2017.
[800] http://search.proquest.com/openview/b33d63e4fad97fd0ada138379cca9549/1?pq-origsite=gscholar&cbl=1819215
[801] https://books.google.com/books?id=C8Iv37Kl-2UC&pg=PA218
[802] https://books.google.com/books?id=hg_Bf1g5KaoC&pg=PA20-IA59e
[803] https://books.google.com/books?id=0NzeDAAAQBAJ
[804] https://books.google.com/books?id=f0fclZ_UjwQC&pg=PA293
[805] https://www.welt.de/debatte/kommentare/article170746305/Kein-Pomp-Keine-Helden-Nirgends-Pracht.html
[806] https://books.google.com/books?id=47iHCwAAQBAJ&pg=PT3
[807] https://books.google.com/books?id=LClEBgAAQBAJ&pg=PA120
[808] http://www.swp.de/ulm/lokales/alb_donau/rommelkaserne-umtaufen-11122818.html
[809] https://books.google.com.vn/books?id=e9znk7vMS-0C&pg=RA12-PR4
[810] https://books.google.com/books?id=GrN-kBGaUwoC&pg=RA1-PR160
[811] https://books.google.com/books/about/Field_Marshal.html?id=u4L3CQAAQBAJ
[812] https://books.google.com/books?id=aCRuuAXx-WkC&pg=PA242
[813] https://www.reuters.com/article/entertainment-us-germany-rommel-idUSBRE8A00RM20121101
[814] https://web.archive.org/web/20161211201550/https://www.reuters.com/article/entertainment-us-germany-rommel-idUSBRE8A00RM20121101
[815] https://web.archive.org/web/20161006014145/https://kuecprd.ku.edu/~upress/cgi-bin/978-0-7006-1791-3.html
[816] https://kuecprd.ku.edu/~upress/cgi-bin/978-0-7006-1791-3.html
[817] http://www.historynet.com/rommels-afrika-korps.htm
[818] https://web.archive.org/web/20161211201703/http://www.historynet.com/rommels-afrika-korps.htm
[819] https://books.google.com/books?id=DW2jAQAAQBAJ&pg=RA1-PA286&lpg=RA1-PA286
[820] https://books.google.com/books?id=bc1DAAAAQBAJ&pg=PA78
[821] http://cpw-online.de/rezensionen/remy.htm
[822] https://web.archive.org/web/20161211201826/http://cpw-online.de/rezensionen/remy.htm
[823] https://books.google.com/books?id=tnIPAQAAMAAJ
[824] https://books.google.com/books?id=luoHDAAAQBAJ&pg=PA381
[825] https://books.google.com/books?id=iHxc8QMgk9cC&pg=PA1861
[826] https://books.google.com/books?id=8l21tdQZmZgC&pg=PA114

[827] https://books.google.com.vn/books?id=7fHnCwAAQBAJ&pg=PA181&dq=rommel+myth&hl=en&sa=X&redir_esc=y#v=onepage&q=rommel%20myth&f=false
[828] http://www.faz.net/aktuell/politik/bundeswehr-augenmass-bei-kasernen-umbenennung-notwendig-15516340.html
[829] http://www.swr.de/rommel/rommel-und-hitler/hitlers-lieblingsgeneral/-/id=10224964/did=10210228/nid=10224964/tmdsxi/index.html
[830] http://www.worldcat.org/search?q=Knight%27s+Cross%3A+A+Life+of+Field+Marshal+Erwin+Rommel+Fraser&qt=owc_search
[831] https//web.archive.org
[832] http://www.spiegel.de/international/germany/world-war-ii-new-research-taints-image-of-desert-fox-rommel-a-484510.html
[833] https://books.google.com/books?id=ihshAQAAIAAJ
[834] https://books.google.com/books?id=nWM9AQAAIAAJ
[835] https://books.google.com/books?id=5qXRAAAAMAAJ
[836] https://books.google.com/books?id=MSF7W-cNQN0C&pg=PA61
[837] https://books.google.com/books?id=5rTWBQAAQBAJ&pg=PA184
[838] https://www.youtube.com/watch?v=VURvlMfdTgg
[839] https://books.google.com/books?id=UPOaw_-o7KUC&pg=PA180
[840] https://books.google.com/books?id=2DaTAwAAQBAJ&pg=PA48
[841] https://books.google.com/books?id=3u-QbCYRV7EC&pg=PA138
[842] http://www.nrhz.de/flyer/beitrag.php?id=23910
[843] https://books.google.com/books?id=mSZyAAAAIAAJ
[844] http://www.swp.de/ulm/lokales/ulm_neu_ulm/Denkmal-des-Anstosses;art4329,1355468
[845] http://www.swp.de/ulm/nachrichten/kultur/bundeswehr_-verminte-geschichte-15016430.html
[846] http://www.bv-opfer-ns-militaerjustiz.de/uploads/Dateien/Presseberichte/JKVerklaerung-und-Aufklaerung20121208.pdf
[847] http://upgr.bv-opfer-ns-militaerjustiz.de/uploads/Dateien/Presseberichte/Tagespost20170520.pdf
[848] https://books.google.com/books?id=QwWtAgAAQBAJ&pg=PT84
[849] https://books.google.com/books?id=lKFaCj-SeTkC&pg=PT54&dq=rommel++gauleiter+Naivit%C3%A4t&hl=en&redir_esc=y
[850] https://books.google.com/books?id=kydwCwAAQBAJ&pg=PT79
[851] https://books.google.com/books?id=fkRGUVbey_wC&pg=PA116
[852] https://books.google.com/books?id=1DLRMQfzyVwC&pg=PA176
[853] https://books.google.com/books?id=bblgexiGhy4C&pg=PA316&lpg=PA316
[854] http://www.swp.de/heidenheim/lokales/heidenheim/feministischer-protest-der-gruenen-am-rommel-denkmal-14562926.html
[855] https://books.google.com/books?id=b-e3DAAAQBAJ&pg=PA15
[856] https://books.google.com.vn/books?id=bflmAAAAMAAJ
[857] http://strategicstudiesinstitute.army.mil/pubs/parameters/articles/1990/1990%20luvaas.pdf
[858] https://books.google.com/books?id=2Wk-AAAAYAAJ
[859] https://books.google.com/books?id=u9JDXgTOgEgC&pg=PA31
[860] //doi.org/10.1093/gerhis/ghn049
[861] https://books.google.com/books?id=diF6jjpgpfgC&pg=PT59
[862] https://books.google.com/books?id=453rHx98crUC&pg=PA25
[863] https://books.google.com/books?id=bBpwCwAAQBAJ&pg=PT97
[864] http://dielinke-lippe.de/nc/presse/aktuell/detail/zurueck/aktuell-24/artikel/warum-umbenennungen-sinnvoll-sind/
[865] https://books.google.com.au/books?id=HBQ3Va075OoC&pg=PA150#v=onepage&q&f=false
[866] https://books.google.com.vn/books?id=lQcv5DesWpIC&pg=PR9&redir_esc=y#v=onepage&q&f=false
[867] http://www.mdr.de/nachrichten/politik/inland/rommel-kaserne-keine-umbenennung-100.html
[868] //www.worldcat.org/issn/1543-7795
[869] //www.jstor.org/stable/2944594
[870] https://books.google.com/books?id=fhMWAwAAQBAJ&pg=PA146

[871] https://www.independent.co.uk/news/world/europe/was-the-desert-fox-an-honest-soldier-or-just-another-nazi-6272076.html
[872] https://books.google.com/books?id=iFDgBQAAQBAJ&pg=PT502
[873] https://www.questia.com/library/journal/1P3-26324710/the-rommel-myth
[874] https://archive.org/details/THEROMMELPAPERS
[875] http://www.faz.net/aktuell/politik/der-erste-weltkrieg/bundeswehr-drei-regeln-fuer-taugliche-vorbilder-15133384.html
[876] https://books.google.com/books?id=qcQLQNxuHfUC&pg=PA238
[877] http://www.paderzeitung.de/index.php?option=com_content&task=view&id=16495&Itemid=240
[878] http//www.westfalen-blatt.de
[879] https://books.google.com/books?id=VcawCwAAQBAJ&pg=PA63
[880] https://books.google.com/books?id=o2Hu9arToqkC&pg=PA33
[881] https://www.swp.de/suedwesten/landkreise/alb-donau/der-name-_rommel_-bleibt-25102772.html
[882] http://trove.nla.gov.au/newspaper/article/42308731
[883] http://www.abc-clio.com/Praeger/product.aspx?pc=C7101C
[884] https//books.google.com.au
[885] https://www.jungewelt.de/m/artikel/304462.das-k%C3%B6nnen-keine-vorbilder-f%C3%BCr-uns-sein.html
[886] https://archive.org/stream/RommelDesmondYoung/Rommel%20-%20Desmond%20Young_djvu.txt
[887] //www.worldcat.org/oclc/48067797
[888] http://www.historynet.com/military-history-january-2016-table-of-contents-2.htm
[889] http://www.historynet.com/march-2016-readers-letters.htm
[890] https://books.google.com/books?id=MWP3AQAAQBAJ&pg=PT62&dq=rommel+%22desert+fox%22+dubbed&hl=en
[891] https://www.telegraph.co.uk/news/worldnews/europe/germany/3836479/Myth-of-humane-Nazi-Erwin-Rommel-debunked.html
[892] https//books.google.com
[893] https://www.welt.de/kultur/article2905248/Erwin-Rommel-Held-der-sauberen-Wehrmacht.html

Article Sources and Contributors

The sources listed for each article provide more detailed licensing information including the copyright status, the copyright owner, and the license conditions.

Erwin Rommel *Source:* https://en.wikipedia.org/w/index.php?oldid=854246733 *License:* Creative Commons Attribution-Share Alike 3.0 *Contributors:* 1997kB, 20DKB03, 72, 786b6364, A D Monroe III, Acroterion, Adamtt9, Alexandervonweimann, Alonso de Mendoza, Alpha Beta Gamma, Ammarpad, Amorymeltzer, Antique Rose, Audaciter, Auntieruth55, AustralianRupert, BD2412, BU Rob13, Babymissfortune, Balon Greyjoy, Berserker276, Beyond My Ken, BiggestSataniaFanboy89, BillC, Brenont, Britmax, Carlotm, Caroca2, Cavalry.charger, Chewings72, Cinderella157, Cloudz679, Clue-Bot NG, DA1, DKong, DMorpheus2, DaddyDevito, Dalliance, Daonguyen95, Darren4444, David in DC, DavidMCEddy, Deamonpen, Display name 99, Dl2000, DocWatson42, Doctorhawkes, Dolphin51, DrVogel, DybrarH, Elijah Isaac Jones, Emiya1980, Erikbiele2005, Erikbiele2017, Erisby, Eye-Truth, Favonian, Ferret, Fishbowl311, Fra Casa, GELongstreet, Gamboler, GeneralizationsAreBad, Gilliam, Gilo1969, Gulumeemee, HandsomeFella, HangingCurve, Henry P. Smith, Historian From Hazarajat, Hohum, HolyT, Home Lander, Howcheng, Hpderuiter2, Ira Leviton, Iridescent, Irondome, Jabberjaw, Jauerback, Jd22292, Jiten D, Joe bideon, John of Reading, Joshmaul, JoshuaSt, JunklinJessy, Jwy, K.e.coffman, Keith D, Kierzek, Kleuske, Knox490, L3X1, LargelyRecyclable, Leggomygreggo8, Little lepidoptera, Lotje, Magioladitis, MarnetteD, Mediatech492, Mfield, Mild Bill Hiccup, Mlgminecrafter5000, Mr Stephen, Mr. Guye, MyMoloboaccount, NZ Footballs Conscience, NickAra123, PamVictor, Parsecboy, Paulturtle, Pavel Vozenilek, Peter West, Phillipenes, Pinacoteca, Primefac, Qaei, Red Jay, Rjensen, Robevans123, Robfwoods, Rupert Nichol, Ryan1783, RyanNavilius5, Sandstein, Schmausschmaus, Serols, Shellwood, SkyWarrior, Sleerning88, Snajamito, Strikerman, Sturmvogel 66, Tdts5, TheGracefulSlick, Tholme, Toddst1, Tony-Ballioni, Trappist the monk, TwoTwoHello, UNSC Luke 1021, Vkt183, White whirlwind, WikiPedant, Yojimbo1941, Zubin12, ΑΔΑ - ΔΑΡ, Виктор Јованоски, 109 anonymous edits 1

Rommel myth *Source:* https://en.wikipedia.org/w/index.php?oldid=851520546 *License:* Creative Commons Attribution-Share Alike 3.0 *Contributors:* *Treker, A D Monroe III, Adpete, Alexb102072, Anotherclown, BDD, Beyond My Ken, Bilsonius, Brandmeister, Brigade Piron, Candido, Catsmoke, Chiswick Chap, Chris troutman, Clifford Mill, Dave souza, David J Johnson, Deamonpen, Dimadick, EdJohnston, Ericoides, Figureofnine, GELongstreet, GeneralizationsAreBad, Gilo1969, GoingBatty, GraemeLeggett, Grassynoel, GreenC, GünniX, Hairy Dude, HeinzCuesta, Henry P. Smith, HolyT, Howcheng, I am One of Many, Ira Leviton, JJMC89, Jabberjaw, Jerodlycett, Jikybebna, Jmcgnh, John of Reading, Johnbod, Jonesey95, JunklinJessy, K.e.coffman, Kierzek, Kjell Knudde, Kypwri, LargelyRecyclable, MPS1992, Magioladitis, MarnetteD, Maunus, Mcc1789, Mr Stephen, Newzild, Nick-D, Orenburg1, P. S. Burton, Pyrope, Seraphimblade, Signedzzz, Thetweaker2017, Trappist the monk, Twofingered Typist, Wnholmes, 31 anonymous edits 73

Image Sources, Licenses and Contributors

The sources listed for each image provide more detailed licensing information including the copyright status, the copyright owner, and the license conditions.

Image *Source:* https://en.wikipedia.org/w/index.php?title=File:Padlock-silver-light.svg *Contributors:* User:AzaToth, User:Eleassar ... 1

Image *Source:* https://en.wikipedia.org/w/index.php?title=File:Bundesarchiv_Bild_146-1977-018-13A,_Erwin_Rommel(brighter).jpg *License:* Creative Commons Attribution-Sharealike 3.0 Germany *Contributors:* Emiya1980, GT1976, Morio ... 1

Image *Source:* https://en.wikipedia.org/w/index.php?title=File:Flag_of_the_German_Empire.svg *License:* Public Domain *Contributors:* User:B1mbo and User:Madden ... 1

Image *Source:* https://en.wikipedia.org/w/index.php?title=File:Flag_of_Germany_(3-2_aspect_ratio).svg *License:* Public Domain *Contributors:* User:Mmxx ... 1

Image *Source:* https://en.wikipedia.org/w/index.php?title=File:Flag_of_German_Reich_(1935–1945).svg *Contributors:* - ... 1

Image *Source:* https://en.wikipedia.org/w/index.php?title=File:Erwin_Rommel_Signature.svg *License:* Public Domain *Contributors:* Badzil, Connormah, Gumruch, McSush, Peeperman, Sarang ... 2

Figure 1 *Source:* https://en.wikipedia.org/w/index.php?title=File:Erwin_Rommel.jpg *License:* anonymous-EU *Contributors:* Alonso de Mendoza, Drdoht, GT1976, Gallop, OgreBot 2, 遼東半島 ... 4

Figure 2 *Source:* https://en.wikipedia.org/w/index.php?title=File:Bundesarchiv_Bild_183-1987-0313-503,_Goslar,_Hitler_schreitet_Ehrenkompanie_ab.jpg *License:* Creative Commons Attribution-Sharealike 3.0 Germany *Contributors:* BotMultichill, Drdoht, Felix Stember, Gkml, Jörg Zägel, Mtsmallwood, Ras67, Teofilo, Thgoiter, YMS ... 7

Figure 3 *Source:* https://en.wikipedia.org/w/index.php?title=File:Bundesarchiv_Bild_101I-013-0064-35,_Polen,_Bormann,_Hitler,_Rommel,_v._Reichenau.jpg *License:* Creative Commons Attribution-Sharealike 3.0 Germany *Contributors:* Andros64, BotMultichill, Cucumber, Drdoht, Frank C. Müller, Gkml, Gorgo, Gunbirddriver2, Jakednb, Jarekt, Martin H., Morio, Mtsmallwood, Nemo5576, Pibwl, Silar, T.seppelt, Teofilo, Thgoiter ... 8

Figure 4 *Source:* https://en.wikipedia.org/w/index.php?title=File:Bundesarchiv_Bild_101I-124-0242-24,_Mosel,_Julius_v._Bernuth,_Erwin_Rommel.jpg *License:* Creative Commons Attribution-Sharealike 3.0 Germany *Contributors:* AnRo0002, Andros64, Blusts, BotMultichill, Cherubino, Christoph Braun, Cobatfor, Drdoht, EWriter, GT1976, Gunbirddriver2, Martin H., Mattes, Morio, Tamba52, Teofilo, Thib Phil, 1 anonymous edits ... 9

Figure 5 *Source:* https://en.wikipedia.org/w/index.php?title=File:Bundesarchiv_Bild_146-1972-045-08,_Westfeldzug,_Rommel_bei_Besprechung_mit_Offizieren.jpg *License:* Creative Commons Attribution-Sharealike 3.0 Germany *Contributors:* AnRo0002, BotMultichill, Bundesarchiv-B6, Cirt, Drdoht, Duch, EWriter, Gunbirddriver2, Morio, Pibwl, Teofilo, Zumalabe, 3 anonymous edits ... 11

Figure 6 *Source:* https://en.wikipedia.org/w/index.php?title=File:WesternDesertBattle_Area1941_en.svg *License:* Creative Commons Attribution-Sharealike 3.0,2.5,2.0,1.0 *Contributors:* Stephen Kirrage talk - contribs ... 13

Figure 7 *Source:* https://en.wikipedia.org/w/index.php?title=File:Bundesarchiv_Bild_101I-783-0109-19,_Nordafrika,_Zugkraftwagen_mit_Flak.2.jpg *License:* Creative Commons Attribution-Sharealike 3.0 Germany *Contributors:* Gunbirddriver2, Morio, Snowdawg ... 14

Figure 8 *Source:* https://en.wikipedia.org/w/index.php?title=File:Bundesarchiv_Bild_101I-783-0150-28,_Nordafrika,_Panzer_III.jpg *License:* Creative Commons Attribution-Sharealike 3.0 Germany *Contributors:* BotMultichill, Bukvoed, Gandvik, Gunbirddriver2, Martin H. ... 15

Figure 9 *Source:* https://en.wikipedia.org/w/index.php?title=File:BattleaxeContestedArea.svg *License:* Creative Commons Attribution-Sharealike 3.0 *Contributors:* Jappalang ... 16

Figure 10 *Source:* https://en.wikipedia.org/w/index.php?title=File:Bundesarchiv_Bild_101I-443-1599-20,_Nordafrika,_bei_Bir_Hacheim,_feuernde_Flak.2.jpg *License:* Creative Commons Attribution-Sharealike 3.0 Germany *Contributors:* Ain92, Gunbirddriver2, Snowdawg ... 17

Figure 11 *Source:* https://en.wikipedia.org/w/index.php?title=File:Bundesarchiv_Bild_183-1982-0927-503,_Bei_El_Agheila,_Rommel_bei_italienischer_Division.jpg *License:* Creative Commons Attribution-Sharealike 3.0 Germany *Contributors:* BotMultichill, Civa61, File Upload Bot (Magnus Manske), G.dallorto, Gunbirddriver2, Maher27777, Martin H., Morio, Teofilo ... 18

Figure 12 *Source:* https://en.wikipedia.org/w/index.php?title=File:Bundesarchiv_Bild_101I-785-0296-22A,_Nordafrika,_Rommel_im_Befehlsfahrzeug_"Greif".jpg *License:* Creative Commons Attribution-Sharealike 3.0 Germany *Contributors:* BotMultichill, Gunbirddriver2, Hohum, Manxruler, Martin H., Morio, Teofilo ... 19

Figure 13 *Source:* https://en.wikipedia.org/w/index.php?title=File:Map_of_siege_of_Tobruk_1942.jpg *License:* Public Domain *Contributors:* United States Military Academy's Department of History ... 20

Figure 14 *Source:* https://en.wikipedia.org/w/index.php?title=File:Bundesarchiv_Bild_101I-785-0293-11,_Tobruk,_Schützenpanzer,_Panzer.jpg *License:* Creative Commons Attribution-Sharealike 3.0 Germany *Contributors:* BotMultichill, Bukvoed, Gunbirddriver2, Hohum, Martin H., SuperTank17, Wieralee ... 22

Figure 15 *Source:* https://en.wikipedia.org/w/index.php?title=File:Bundesarchiv_Bild_146-1973-012-43,_Erwin_Rommel.jpg *License:* Creative Commons Attribution-Sharealike 3.0 Germany *Contributors:* A1B2C3D4, Alonso de Mendoza, Berliner Schildkröte, BotMultichill, Bundesarchiv-B6, DIREKTOR, Denniss, FDMS4, Felix Stember, GT1976, Lupus in Saxonia, Morio, Ruffneck88, Teofilo, VanKleinen, 1 anonymous edits ... 22

Figure 16 *Source:* https://en.wikipedia.org/w/index.php?title=File:Alamein1st1942_07.svg *License:* Creative Commons Attribution-Sharealike 3.0 *Contributors:* Kirrages ... 24

Figure 17 *Source:* https://en.wikipedia.org/w/index.php?title=File:Bundesarchiv_Bild_101I-784-0249-04A,_Nordafrika,_Rommel_im_Befehlsfahrzeug_"Greif".2.jpg *License:* Creative Commons Attribution-Sharealike 3.0 Germany *Contributors:* Gunbirddriver2, Morio ... 25

Figure 18 *Source:* https://en.wikipedia.org/w/index.php?title=File:Destroyed_Panzer_IIIs_near_Tel_el_Eisa_1942.jpg *License:* Public Domain *Contributors:* Australian armed forces ... 26

Figure 19 *Source:* https://en.wikipedia.org/w/index.php?title=File:2_Battle_of_El_Alamein_010.png *License:* GNU Free Documentation License *Contributors:* Noclador ... 27

Figure 20 *Source:* https://en.wikipedia.org/w/index.php?title=File:Bundesarchiv_Bild_146-1990-071-31,_Nordafrika,_Rommel,_Bayerlein.jpg *License:* Creative Commons Attribution-Sharealike 3.0 Germany *Contributors:* BotMultichill, Bukvoed, Catsmeat, Florival fr, Gunbirddriver2, Hohum, K.e.coffman, Morio, Moumou82, Pibwl, Ras67, Rcbutcher, SuperTank17, Teofilo, 1 anonymous edits ... 29

Figure 21 *Source:* https://en.wikipedia.org/w/index.php?title=File:Bundesarchiv_Bild_101I-300-1863-29,_Riva-Bella,_Waffenvorführung_Panzerwerfer,_Rommel.jpg *License:* Creative Commons Attribution-Sharealike 3.0 Germany *Contributors:* BotMultichill, Bukvoed, Gunbirddriver2, Martin H., Morio, Teofilo, Иван Дулин, 1 anonymous edits ... 31

Figure 22 *Source:* https://en.wikipedia.org/w/index.php?title=File:Bundesarchiv_Bild_101I-719-0240-35,_Pas_de_Calais,_Atlantikwall,_Luftlandehindernisse.jpg *License:* Creative Commons Attribution-Sharealike 3.0 Germany *Contributors:* Alonso de Mendoza, BotMultichill, KuK, Llorenzi, Martin H., TCY, Teofilo, Vdv-r31 ... 32

Figure 23 *Source:* https://en.wikipedia.org/w/index.php?title=File:Bundesarchiv_Bild_101I-300-1863-33A,_Riva-Bella,_Waffenvorführung_Panzerwerfer,_Rommel.jpg *License:* Creative Commons Attribution-Sharealike 3.0 Germany *Contributors:* Ain92, BotMultichill, Bukvoed, Felix Stember, Gunbirddriver2, Martin H., Morio, Teofilo, 1 anonymous edits ... 33

Figure 24 *Source:* https://en.wikipedia.org/w/index.php?title=File:Bundesarchiv_Bild_101I-718-0149-12A,_Paris,_Rommel,_von_Rundstedt,_Gause_und_Zimmermann.jpg *License:* Creative Commons Attribution-Sharealike 3.0 Germany *Contributors:* BotMultichill, Drdoht, Fallschirmjäger, GT1976, Martin H., Morio, Oneblackline, Teofilo ... 34

Figure 25 *Source:* https://en.wikipedia.org/w/index.php?title=File:Bundesarchiv_Bild_146-1972-025-10,_Hitler-Attentat,_20._Juli_1944.jpg *License:* Creative Commons Attribution-Sharealike 3.0 Germany *Contributors:* BotMultichill, Cantons-de-l'Est, Drdoht, Frank C. Müller, MOSZCZ, MisterBee1966, Mtsmallwood, Wolfmann, YMS, 5 anonymous edits ... 36

Figure 26 *Source:* https://en.wikipedia.org/w/index.php?title=File:Bundesarchiv_Bild_183-J30704,_Ulm,_Beisetzung_Rommel.jpg *License:* Creative Commons Attribution-Sharealike 3.0 Germany *Contributors:* Ain92, BotMultichill, Burts, Cathy Richards, Concord, Cycn, Drdoht, Eddaido, Gunbirddriver2, Ies, Jacklee, Liesel, Mindmatrix, Morio, Neelix, Olybrius, Pibwl, Teofilo, Wolfmann, 3 anonymous edits ... 38

Figure 27 *Source:* https://en.wikipedia.org/w/index.php?title=File:Rommels-grab.jpg *License:* GNU Free Documentation License *Contributors:* Tatjana8047 ... 40

Figure 28 *Source:* https://en.wikipedia.org/w/index.php?title=File:Bundesarchiv_Bild_183-B20800,_Nordafrika,_Rommel_und_Westphal_schieben_Auto.jpg *License:* Creative Commons Attribution-Sharealike 3.0 Germany *Contributors:* Alonso de Mendoza, BotMultichill, Drdoht, High Contrast, Martin H., Morio, RomanM82, Teofilo ... 41

Figure 29 *Source:* https://en.wikipedia.org/w/index.php?title=File:Bundesarchiv_Bild_146-1977-017-10A,_Nordafrika,_Rommel_mit_Offizieren.jpg *License:* Creative Commons Attribution-Sharealike 3.0 Germany *Contributors:* Alonso de Mendoza, BotMultichill, Manxruler, Morio, Teofilo 43

Figure 30 *Source:* https://en.wikipedia.org/w/index.php?title=File:Bundesarchiv_Bild_101I-785-0299-24A,_Tobruk,_Rommel,_Bayerlein,_englische_Kriegsgefangene.2.jpg *License:* Creative Commons Attribution-Sharealike 3.0 Germany *Contributors:* Gunbirddriver2, Manxruler, Morio, Zumalabe ... 45

Figure 31 *Source:* https://en.wikipedia.org/w/index.php?title=File:Bundesarchiv_Bild_146-1970-076-43,_Paris,_Erwin_Rommel_bei_Siegesparade.jpg *License:* Creative Commons Attribution-Sharealike 3.0 Germany *Contributors:* Alonso de Mendoza, AnRo0002, BotMultichill, Drdoht, GT1976, Jakednb, Morio, Para, Teofilo, 2 anonymous edits 49
Figure 32 *Source:* https://en.wikipedia.org/w/index.php?title=File:Bundesarchiv_Bild_101I-719-0243-33,_Atlantikwall,_Inspektion_Erwin_Rommel_mit_Offizieren.jpg *License:* Creative Commons Attribution-Sharealike 3.0 Germany *Contributors:* BotMultichill, Gunbirddriver2, Llorenzi, Manxruler, Martin H., Morio, TCY, Tekstman, Teofilo 51
Figure 33 *Source:* https://en.wikipedia.org/w/index.php?title=File:Bundesarchiv_Bild_146-1977-119-08,_Erwin_Rommel,_Adolf_Hitler.jpg *License:* Creative Commons Attribution-Sharealike 3.0 Germany *Contributors:* Alonso de Mendoza, BotMultichill, Morio, Mtsmallwood, Teofilo, YMS 53
Figure 34 *Source:* https://en.wikipedia.org/w/index.php?title=File:Rommel's_Africa_uniform.jpg *License:* Public Domain *Contributors:* Mister-Bee1966 (talk) 59
Figure 35 *Source:* https://en.wikipedia.org/w/index.php?title=File:Busto_Rommel.jpg *License:* Creative Commons Attribution 2.5 *Contributors:* Aizga, Ashashyou, JMCC1, Morio 64
Image *Source:* https://en.wikipedia.org/w/index.php?title=File:Symbol_support_vote.svg *License:* Public Domain *Contributors:* Anomie, Fastily, Jo-Jo Eumerus 73
Figure 36 *Source:* https://en.wikipedia.org/w/index.php?title=File:Bundesarchiv_Bild_146-1970-076-43,_Paris,_Erwin_Rommel_bei_Siegesparade.jpg *License:* Creative Commons Attribution-Sharealike 3.0 Germany *Contributors:* Alonso de Mendoza, AnRo0002, BotMultichill, Drdoht, GT1976, Jakednb, Morio, Para, Teofilo, 2 anonymous edits 75
Figure 37 *Source:* https://en.wikipedia.org/w/index.php?title=File:Bundesarchiv_Bild_101I-719-0243-33,_Atlantikwall,_Inspektion_Erwin_Rommel_mit_Offizieren.jpg *License:* Creative Commons Attribution-Sharealike 3.0 Germany *Contributors:* BotMultichill, Gunbirddriver2, Llorenzi, Manxruler, Martin H., Morio, TCY, Tekstman, Teofilo 78
Figure 38 *Source:* https://en.wikipedia.org/w/index.php?title=File:Bundesarchiv_Bild_183-B20800,_Nordafrika,_Rommel_und_Westphal_schieben_Auto.jpg *License:* Creative Commons Attribution-Sharealike 3.0 Germany *Contributors:* Alonso de Mendoza, BotMultichill, Drdoht, High Contrast, Martin H., Morio, RomanM82, Teofilo 83
Figure 39 *Source:* https://en.wikipedia.org/w/index.php?title=File:Bundesarchiv_Bild_183-1987-0313-503,_Goslar,_Hitler_schreitet_Ehrenkompanie_ab.jpg *License:* Creative Commons Attribution-Sharealike 3.0 Germany *Contributors:* BotMultichill, Drdoht, Felix Stember, Gkml, Jörg Zägel, Mtsmallwood, Ras67, Teofilo, Thgoiter, YMS 84
Figure 40 *Source:* https://en.wikipedia.org/w/index.php?title=File:Bundesarchiv_Bild_101I-013-0064-35,_Polen,_Bormann,_Hitler,_Rommel,_v._Reichenau.jpg *License:* Creative Commons Attribution-Sharealike 3.0 Germany *Contributors:* BotMultichill, Drdoht, Felix Stember, Gkml, Gorgo, Gunbirddriver2, Jakednb, Jarekt, Martin H., Morio, Mtsmallwood, Nemo5576, Pibwl, Silar, T.seppelt, Teofilo, Thgoiter 85
Figure 41 *Source:* https://en.wikipedia.org/w/index.php?title=File:Bundesarchiv_Bild_146-1977-119-08,_Erwin_Rommel,_Adolf_Hitler.jpg *License:* Creative Commons Attribution-Sharealike 3.0 Germany *Contributors:* Alonso de Mendoza, BotMultichill, Morio, Mtsmallwood, Teofilo, YMS 87
Figure 42 *Source:* https://en.wikipedia.org/w/index.php?title=File:Bundesarchiv_Bild_101I-443-1582-32,_Nordafrika,_Generaloberst_Erwin_Rommel.jpg *License:* Creative Commons Attribution-Sharealike 3.0 Germany *Contributors:* BotMultichill, Martin H., Mogelzahn, Morio, Ras67, Teofilo, Thgoiter, Tsui 93
Figure 43 *Source:* https://en.wikipedia.org/w/index.php?title=File:Senne.jpg *License:* GNU Free Documentation License *Contributors:* User:Nikater 97

License

Creative Commons Attribution-Share Alike 3.0
//creativecommons.org/licenses/by-sa/3.0/

Index

Accordion, 47
Adolf Heusinger, 79
Adolf Hitler, 3, 6, 7, 56, 73, 74, 84
Afrika Korps, 2, 88
Alan Cunningham, 17
Albert Kesselring, 17, 86, 118, 123
Alexander Neu, 98
Alexander von Falkenhausen, 36, 91
Alfred Gause, 56
Alfred Ingemar Berndt, 49, 75
Alfred Jodl, 87
Allan R. Millett, 94
Allen Dulles, 36, 91
Allies of World War II, 3, 73
Alpenkorps (German Empire), 5
Angus Calder, 83
Antisemitism, 3
Antony Beevor, 74
Archibald Wavell, 13, 61, 80
Ariel Sharon, 61
Arminius, 97
Army Group Africa, 2
Army Group B, 2, 30
Army Group E, 30
Army of Württemberg, 1
Arras, 10
Atlantic Wall, 31, 32, 51, 77, 78
Attack on Pearl Harbor, 76
Avesnes, 10
Axis powers, 73

Baden-Württemberg, 65
Baldur von Schirach, 6, 85
Basil Liddell Hart, 41, 58, 74, 79
Battle for France, 11
Battle of Alam el Halfa, 25
Battle of Alam Halfa, 2
Battle of Arras (1940), 2, 10
Battle of Bir Hakeim, 2, 21
Battle of Caporetto, 2, 5, 65
Battle of El Agheila, 2
Battle of France, 2, 3, 74
Battle of Gazala, 2, 20
Battle of Greece, 14

Battle of Kasserine Pass, 76
Battle of Medenine, 2, 29
Battle of Singapore, 21
Battle of the Kasserine Pass, 2, 29
Belisarius, 88
Benghazi, 14
Berkley Publishing Group, 105
Bernard Montgomery, 61, 74
Bernard Montgomery, 1st Viscount Montgomery of Alamein, 24
Bersaglieri, 44
B. H. Liddell Hart, 69, 81, 105
Blitzkrieg, 81
Bonner Fellers, 20
Brian Horrocks, 25, 88
British Eighth Army, 17
British Empire, 77
British Indian Army, 79
British propaganda during World War II, 73, 76
Bundeswehr, 58, 61, 80

Caesar von Hofacker, 92
Cambridge University Press, 100, 102, 105
Carl Goerdeler, 36, 91
Carl Heinrich von Stülpnagel, 36, 91
Carl Peters, 82
Case White, 87
Caucasus, 23
Chaim ibn Attar, 44
Charles Douglas-Home (journalist), 67
Charles F. Marshall, 47, 71
Charles NTchoréré, 12
Charley Fox, 35
Cherbourg, 11
Chief of Staff, Bundeswehr, 61, 89
Chivalry, 3, 92
Chronological items, 83
CITEREFAddington1967, 119, 123
CITEREFAlexander2012, 108
CITEREFAmbrose1994, 113
CITEREFArquilla1996, 114
CITEREFAtkinson2002, 123
CITEREFAtkinson2013, 115, 123
CITEREFAustin2004, 123

CITEREFBall2016, 117, 123
CITEREFBarnett1989, 114, 124
CITEREFBarr2014, 116, 120
CITEREFBartels2017, 125
CITEREFBattistelli2012, 122, 124
CITEREFBaxter2014, 123, 124
CITEREFBeckett2013, 114
CITEREFBeckett2014, 108, 109, 112, 114, 115, 117, 118, 120, 123
CITEREFBeevor2009, 115
CITEREFBeevor2012, 120
CITEREFBenishay2016, 115
CITEREFBlumenson2001, 124
CITEREFBlumentritt1952, 117
CITEREFBöhmer2012, 125
CITEREFBoog2001, 123
CITEREFBradford2011, 118
CITEREFBrighton2008, 111, 114, 117, 124
CITEREFBrighton2009, 124
CITEREFButler2015, 107–119, 122–124
CITEREFButler2016, 107
CITEREFCaddick-Adams1998, 114
CITEREFCaddick-Adams2012, 108, 116–118, 120–123
CITEREFCaddick-Adams2013, 112
CITEREFCalder2012, 122
CITEREFCarver1962, 111
CITEREFCarver2005, 107
CITEREFCeva1990, 121
CITEREFChambers2012, 121
CITEREFChurchill1950, 117
CITEREFCitino2007, 125
CITEREFCitino2012, 116, 119, 120, 122, 123
CITEREFCocks2012, 114
CITEREFCoetzee2013, 124
CITEREFCoggins1980, 111, 114
CITEREFCohen2015, 115
CITEREFColin2012, 115
CITEREFConnelly2009, 124
CITEREFConnelly2014, 118, 122
CITEREFCreveld1977, 123
CITEREFDäniker2002, 118
CITEREFDetsch2002, 124
CITEREFDeuel1943, 121
CITEREFDixon2016, 124
CITEREFDouglas-Home1973, 109–111
CITEREFDoweHecht2016, 124
CITEREFDuffyRicci2013, 122
CITEREFEchternkamp2010, 120
CITEREFEdwards2012, 124
CITEREFEvans2009, 113, 115, 124
CITEREFFaltin2014, 112
CITEREFFAZ2018, 125
CITEREFFinklestone2013, 119
CITEREFFischer2014, 124
CITEREFFraser1993, 107–111, 119, 122

CITEREFFriedmann2007, 118, 122
CITEREFGabel2014, 124
CITEREFGiordano2000, 125
CITEREFGiordano2010, 124
CITEREFGoldschmidt Waldeck1943, 121
CITEREFGrossman1993, 107
CITEREFHachten WeeWee2004, 122
CITEREFHagen2014, 125
CITEREFHamilton2012, 122
CITEREFHanley2008, 123
CITEREFHansen2014, 112, 115, 118, 124
CITEREFHart2014, 107, 112, 123, 124
CITEREFHartmann2011, 123
CITEREFHecht2008, 125
CITEREFHecht (editor)2008, 115
CITEREFHeiducoff2017, 125
CITEREFHoffmann2004, 107–112, 114
CITEREFHolderfieldVarhola2009, 115
CITEREFHolles1945, 121
CITEREFHolmes2009, 118
CITEREFHouse1985, 107
CITEREFKanold2017, 125
CITEREFKitchen2009, 115, 116, 118, 120–122
CITEREFKitchen2014, 125
CITEREFKnab1999, 125
CITEREFKnab2017, 125
CITEREFKnopp2011, 113
CITEREFKnopp2013, 112, 118, 120
CITEREFKnorr2015, 123
CITEREFKnox2000, 123
CITEREFKrausePhillips2006, 123
CITEREFKrausePhillips2007, 108
CITEREFKubetzky2010, 117, 120
CITEREFKummer2017, 125
CITEREFLatimer2002, 114, 115, 124
CITEREFLeithäuser2017, 125
CITEREFLevine1999, 123
CITEREFLevine2007, 123
CITEREFLewin1998, 107–111, 114, 115, 122, 123
CITEREFLieb2013, 114, 124
CITEREFLieb2014, 111–116, 119, 121, 123
CITEREFLuvaas1990, 118, 122
CITEREFMacksey1979, 125
CITEREFMaier2013, 108, 122
CITEREFMajdalany2003, 115, 124
CITEREFMajor2008, 117, 118, 120–122, 124
CITEREFMarshall1994, 112–115, 117, 124
CITEREFMass2006, 120, 122
CITEREFMcMahon2014, 124
CITEREFMDR2017, 125
CITEREFMearsheimer1988, 118, 122
CITEREFMegargee2000, 119, 123
CITEREFMenne2017, 125

CITEREFMessenger2009, 108, 111, 112, 114–116, 122
CITEREFMitcham1997, 111–113
CITEREFMitcham2007, 109, 112, 114, 119
CITEREFMitcham2007a, 123
CITEREFMitcham2007b, 123
CITEREFMitcham2008, 109
CITEREFMitcham2009, 119
CITEREFMitcham2014, 117
CITEREFMitcham, Jr.1997, 124
CITEREFMitcham, Jr.2007a, 124
CITEREFMoorhouse2007, 119
CITEREFMurray1995, 122
CITEREFMurray2009, 124
CITEREFMurray2011, 122
CITEREFMurrayMillett2009, 108, 113
CITEREFNaumann2009, 112, 116–118, 122–124
CITEREFNeitzel2005, 124
CITEREFPerry2012, 115
CITEREFPimlott1994, 108
CITEREFPimlott2003, 107, 108, 112, 113
CITEREFPimlott2014, 124
CITEREFPlayfair1960, 110
CITEREFPorch2004, 113, 114, 119
CITEREFPyta2015, 117, 120, 124
CITEREFRemy2002, 107, 109, 112–119, 122, 124
CITEREFRemy2012, 122
CITEREFRemy2015, 107
CITEREFReuth2005, 107, 112, 116, 117, 120–124
CITEREFRice2009, 111–113, 115
CITEREFRobinson1997, 120
CITEREFRommel1982, 110, 111, 113, 114, 116, 117
CITEREFRommelLiddell Hart1953, 120
CITEREFRotte2017, 125
CITEREFSadkovich2003, 125
CITEREFSadler2016, 118
CITEREFScheck2006, 109
CITEREFScheck2010, 107
CITEREFScherzer2007, 119
CITEREFSchmitt2017, 125
CITEREFSchnadwinkel2017, 125
CITEREFSchrijvers1997, 121
CITEREFSearle2014, 107, 108, 115, 117, 121, 122
CITEREFShepherd2016, 115
CITEREFShirer1960, 110, 112, 113, 123
CITEREFShowalter2006, 107, 114, 117, 122, 124
CITEREFSmelserDavies2008, 121
CITEREFStickler2005, 124
CITEREFStone2009, 108
CITEREFStrawson2014, 118
CITEREFStroud2013, 123
CITEREFSWP2018, 125
CITEREFThe Cairns Post1941, 121
CITEREFTime1951, 121
CITEREFvom Hagen2014, 118
CITEREFVon FleischhauerFriedmann2012, 107, 113–115
CITEREFvon Luck1989, 110, 114
CITEREFvon Mellenthin1956, 113, 114
CITEREFWaldeck1943, 122
CITEREFWatson1999, 108, 111, 114–118, 120–124
CITEREFWatson2006, 117, 124
CITEREFWette2007, 121
CITEREFWillmott1984, 111, 112
CITEREFWistrich2001, 118
CITEREFWrobel2017, 125
CITEREFYoung1950, 112, 114, 120
CITEREFZabecki2016, 108, 118, 122, 123
CITEREFZabecki March2016, 119, 123
CITEREFZaloga2013, 108, 112, 116
Clasp to the Iron Cross, 65
Claude Auchinleck, 16, 61, 76
Claus von Stauffenberg, 36
Clean Wehrmacht, 59, 82
Cold War, 73
Colin Smith (journalist), 82
Colonial Order of the Star of Italy, 65
Commando Order, 45
Commonwealth of Nations, 21
Cornell University Press, 103
Correlli Barnett, 78
Counterpropaganda, 74
Cyanide pill, 3
Cyanide poisoning, 39

Daily Express, 76
Daniel Allen Butler, 66, 89, 99
Danzig, 4
David Fraser (British Army officer), 67, 81, 101
David Irving, 95
David T. Zabecki, 61, 84, 88, 106, 118, 123
D-Day, 33
Death mask, 59
De:Haus der Geschichte Baden-Württemberg, 32
De:Maurice Philip Remy, 69
Dennis Showalter, 105
De:Raffael Scheck, 6
Der Spiegel, 39, 54, 59, 82, 115
Desert Air Force, 19
De:Siegfried Storbeck, 60
Deutsches Afrika Korps, 13
Deutsches Historisches Museum, 71
Dieppe, 11

Die Welt, 55, 106
Digital object identifier, 68, 103
Dinant, 74
Disputed statement, 84
Douglas Porch, 62, 69
Dresden, 6
Drumhead court-martial, 38
Dunkirk evacuation, 11

Eastern Front (World War II), 23
Echternkamp, Jörg, 101
Edgar Trost, 62
Edmund Roszczynialski, 46
Eduard Dietl, 48
Egypt, 65
El Agheila, 14, 18, 19
El Alamein, 23
Embolism, 39
Ensign (rank), 4
Eric Dorman-Smith, 57
Erich Marcks, 33
Erich von Manstein, 37
Ernest Bevin, 80
Ernst Jünger, 54
Ernst Maisel, 39
Erwin Rommel, **1**, 73
Erwin von Witzleben, 36
Ettore Bastico, 90

Fähnrich, 4
Fall Rot, 11
Federal Ministry of Defence (Germany), 98
Federal Republic of Germany, 3, 73
Field marshal, 2
Field Marshal Rommel Barracks, Augustdorf, 3, 65, 98
Field Marshal Rommel Barracks, Osterode, 65
First Battle of El Alamein, 2, 23
First Battle of the Argonne, 2
Flak, 10
Fort Capuzzo, 16
Fortress Europe, 50, 77
Founding of Rome, 44
France, 4
Franz Halder, 14, 56, 87
Fr:Dominque Lormier, 12
Friedrich Paulus, 15, 56
Friedrich Ruge, 31
Friedrich von Mellenthin, 42, 68, 90
Fritz Bayerlein, 16, 81
Friuli Venezia Giulia, 65
Führerbegleitbrigade, 7, 86
Führer Headquarters, 49, 76
Führersonderzug, 7

Gastone Gambara, 17

Gau Württemberg-Hohenzollern, 1
Generalfeldmarschall, 1, 2
Generalleutnant, 13
Generalmajor, 7, 86
Geoffrey P. Megargee, 62, 88, 104
George S. Patton, 61
Georg-Hans Reinhardt, 10
Georg Stumme, 26, 41
Gerd von Rundstedt, 10, 34, 38, 48
German Army (Wehrmacht), 1
German counterattacks, 30
German destroyer Rommel, 65
German Empire, 1, 3
German National Library of Economics, 72
German Navy, 65
German resistance to Nazism, 35, 91
German Tank Museum, 59
Gertrud Stemmer, 2
Giovanni Messe, 29
Giuseppe Civati, 65
Gold Medal of Military Valour, 65
Goslar, 6
Greece, 30
Guido Knopp, 74

Hagiography, 79
Halfaya Pass, 16
Hans-Jürgen von Arnim, 29
Hans Speidel, 3, 36, 58, 70, 79
Hans-Ulrich Wehler, 59
Hans von Luck, 68
Harold Alexander, 24
HarperCollins, 101
Hartmut Bagger, 62
Harvard University Press, 106
Hauptmann, 5
Heidenheim an der Brenz, 1, 3
Heinrich Eberbach, 35, 92
Heinrich Himmler, 93
Heinrich Kirchheim, 16, 38
Heinz Guderian, 10, 38
Helmut Willmann, 62
Hendrik Klopper, 21
Hermann Hoth, 10
Herrlingen, 1
Himmerod memorandum, 79
Historikerstreit, 95
History, 47
History, society, and culture, 48
History (U.S. TV channel), 113
Hitler Youth, 6, 85
HMSO, 69
Hobarts Funnies, 32
Holocaust, 46
Horst Boog, 90
House of Commons of the United Kingdom, 87

136

Houx, 74
Hradčany, 53
Hugh Trevor-Roper, 80

Ian Stanley Ord Playfair, 69
Infanterie greift an, 6, 74
Infantry Attacks, 2
Infiltration tactics, 5
International Standard Book Number, 66–71, 98–106, 115
International Standard Serial Number, 104
Internet Archive, 71
Invasion of Normandy, 2, 3
Invasion of Poland, 2, 7, 86
Iron Cross, 2, 5, 64
Isoroku Yamamoto, 63
I SS Panzer Corps, 32
Italian Campaign (World War I), 4
Italian Front (World War I), 2, 5
Italian XX Motorized Corps, 17
Italo Gariboldi, 13

Jack Coggins, 66
Jacob wrestling with the angel, 44
Jäger (infantry), 6
James Mason, 81
James Ramsay Montagu Butler, 69
J. C. Squire, 82
Johann von Ravenstein, 16
John Hackett (British Army officer), 82
John Mearsheimer, 58, 81, 103
Jon Latimer, 68, 103
Jörg Echternkamp, 74
Jörg Müllner, 95
Joseph Goebbels, 48, 49, 75
JSTOR, 104
Julian Thompson (Royal Marines officer), 71
Jürgen Heiducoff, 96

Kangaroo court, 38
Karl Hanke, 49, 75
Karl Strölin, 35, 91
Karl von Luz, 3
Kingdom of Italy, 13
Kingdom of Württemberg, 1, 3
Klaus Naumann, 61, 69, 89, 93, 104, 117, 118, 123, 124
Knights Cross of the Iron Cross, 65
Knights Cross of the Iron Cross with Oak Leaves, Swords and Diamonds, 2
Knights Cross with Oak Leaves, 65
Knights Cross with Oak Leaves and Swords, 65
Knights Cross with Oak Leaves, Swords and Diamonds, 65
Kolovrat (mountain ridge), 5
Konrad Adenauer, 79

Konstantin von Neurath, 36, 91
Korean War, 78

Labour Party (UK), 80
Lake Garda, 30
Lawrence of Arabia, 58, 81
LeMO, 71
Leo Geyr von Schweppenburg, 33
Leslie Morshead, 15
Libya, 13
Lieutenant, 4
Lieutenant General, 15
Lille, 10
Lindau, 6
Logarithm tables, 7
Longarone, 5
Ludwig Crüwell, 16
Lütjens-class destroyer, 65

M3 Lee, 20
M4 Sherman, 27
MacGregor Knox, 90
Malcolm Muggeridge, 80
Malta, 20
Manfred Rommel, 2, 40, 64, 113
Manfred von Richthofen, 96
Mareth Line, 29
Margival, 35
Mark Connelly, 81, 100
Martin Blumenson, 63
Martin Bormann, 8, 92
Martin Kitchen, 47, 67, 75, 102, 121
Martin van Creveld, 88, 100
Matajur, 5
Matilda II, 10
Matilda Mk I, 10
Matthias Stickler, 95
Maurice Philip Remy, 74, 92, 104
Mersa El Brega, 14
Mersa Matruh, 23, 65
Metanarrative, 94
Meuse, 74
Michael Wolffsohn, 97
Middle East, 23
Middle East Command, 13
Miles Christianus, 62
Military Merit Order (Württemberg), 64
Military Review, 71, 105
Moshe Dayan, 61
Munster, Lower Saxony, 59
Myth, 74
Myth of the clean Wehrmacht, 73, 81

National Socialism, 73, 83
NATO, 3, 58, 80
Naval War College, 70

Nazi Germany, 1, 2, 73
Nazi ideology, 3
Nazi Party, 53, 83
Nazi Party Chancellery, 92
Nazi propaganda, 3, 48, 73, 75
Nazi rise to power, 53
Nazi seizure of power, 3, 83
Nazism and the Wehrmacht, 80
Neil Ritchie, 18
Neue Deutsche Biographie, 71
New York City, New York, 105
Nigel Hamilton (author), 71, 84, 101, 106
No. 412 Squadron RCAF, 35
Normandy, 30
Norman F. Dixon, 93
Norman Ohler, 48
Norman Schwarzkopf, Jr., 61
North African Campaign, 2, 3, 74

Oberkommando der Wehrmacht, 13
Oberkommando des Heeres, 11
Oberleutnant, 5
Oberst, 7
Oberstleutnant, 6
OCLC, 66, 70, 106
OKH, 50, 62, 77
OKW, 62, 88
Opel, 39
Operation Achse, 30
Operational art, 61
Operation Barbarossa, 15, 49, 76
Operation Battleaxe, 2, 16
Operation Brevity, 2, 16
Operation Compass, 13
Operation Crusader, 2, 17
Operation Flipper, 63
Operation Fortitude, 33
Operation Gaff, 63
Operation Herkules, 23
Operation Sea Lion, 11
Operation Sonnenblume, 2, 13
Organisation Todt, 47
Owen Connelly, 41

Palgrave Macmillan, 68, 104
Panzer, 86
Panzer Army Africa, 2, 20
Panzer division, 8
Panzer II, 20
Panzer III, 15, 26
Panzer-Lehr-Division, 34
Panzerschlachten, 68
Paris, 30
Pas-de-Calais, 32
Patrick Major, 68, 79, 103, 118
Paul Hausser, 37

Paul von Lettow-Vorbeck, 82
Peoples Court (German), 38
Peter Caddick-Adams, 53, 66, 78, 84, 99, 116, 121
Peter Lieb, 62, 74, 103, 116, 121
Plot against Hitler, 3
Pour le Mérite, 2, 5, 64
Praeger Publishers, 70, 105
Protezione Civile, 65

Qattara Depression, 23

Ralf Georg Reuth, 84, 104
Ralph Rotte, 96
Randall Hansen, 52, 101
RCAF, 35
Reich Chancellery, 8
Reich Ministry of Propaganda, 75
Reich Propaganda Ministry, 49, 75
Reichsheer, 1
Reinhard Heydrich, 63
Reuters, 95
R. G. Waldeck, 82
Richard Crossman, 80
Richard J. Evans, 46, 67, 91, 101
Richard Overy, 94
Rick Atkinson, 47, 86, 87
River Meuse, 10
River Seine, 11
River Somme, 33
Robert Citino, 53, 62, 66, 70, 84, 100, 118
Roland Freisler, 38
Romania during World War I, 2
Romanian Campaign (World War I), 4
Rommel Barracks, Dornstadt, 65
Rommel (film), 60
Rommel Museum, Blaustein, 65
Rommel Museum, Mersa Matruh, 65
Rommel myth, 3, 56, **73**
Rommels asparagus, 32
Rommel: The Desert Fox, 58, 73, 79
Romulus, 44
Ronald Lewin, 81
Ronald Smelser, 105
Rouen, 11

Sainte-Foy-de-Montgommery, 35
Salient (military), 27
Samuel W. Mitcham, 89, 104
Schwäbisch Gmünd, 6
Sd.Kfz. 250, 19, 25
SdKfz 6, 14
Second Battle of El Alamein, 2, 26, 27, 77
Second Battle of Oituz, 5
Sepp Dietrich, 37, 48
Sic, 79

Siege, 15
Siege of Lille (1940), 2, 10
Siege of Tobruk, 2, 15
Siegfried Westphal, 19, 90
Sieg im Westen, 75
Sippenhaft, 39
Sirte, 13
Sollum, 16
Sönke Neitzel, 71, 92, 104
Southern Germany, 3
Soviet Union, 76
Spiegel Online, 67, 101, 118, 122
Spitfire, 35
Stackpole Books, 68, 100, 103, 105
State funeral, 40
Steven Zaloga, 63
Strategic Studies Institute, 68, 103
Sturmabteilung, 83
Suez Canal, 23
Suicide, 3, 38
Sun Li-jen, 61
Swabian German, 42
Sword Beach, 31
Szymon Datner, 45

Taylor & Francis, 100
Terry Brighton, 66, 118
Teutoburg Forest, 97
The Cairns Post, 76
The Daily Telegraph, 80, 106
The Desert Fox: The Story of Rommel, 80
The Desert Rats (film), 81
The Greens, 97
The Holocaust, 3
The Left (Germany), 98
The Myth of the Eastern Front, 105
The National WWII Museum, 71, 84, 101, 106
Theresian Military Academy, 7
The Third Reich at War, 67, 101
The Wehrmacht: History, Myth, Reality, 106
Third Reich, 3, 56
Thomas Vogel (historian), 87
Time (magazine), 80, 98
Timimi, 19
Tobruk, 15
Ton van Loon, 98
Trench warfare, 5
Tripoli, 13
Tunisia, 28
Tunisian Campaign, 76
Types 952 and 956, 41

Ulm, 3, 40
Ultra, 14, 26
Ultra (cryptography), 30
United Kingdom, 3

United States, 3
United States Naval Institute, 61, 88
Unity of command, 61, 89
University Press of Kansas, 70, 100
U.S. II Corps, 29
USNI, 89
US State Department, 20

Waffen-SS, 46
Walburga Stemmer, 63
Walther Rauff, 46
Walther von Brauchitsch, 48
War in History, 71
Wehrmacht, 2, 42, 73, 79
Weimar Republic, 1
Weingarten, Württemberg, 4
Wesley Clark, 61
Western Desert Campaign, 13
Western Desert Force, 14
Wiederbewaffnung, 3, 57, 73
Wiener Neustadt, 7
Wilhelm Bittrich, 37
Wilhelm Burgdorf, 39
Wilhelm Keitel, 38, 87
William Gott, 24
William L. Shirer, 70, 105
Williamson Murray, 94
Winston Churchill, 66
Wolf Heckmann, 61, 82, 88
Wolfram Pyta, 74
Wolfram Wette, 106
WorldCat, 71
World War I, 2, 57, 74
World War II, 2

XIII Corps (United Kingdom), 17
XIII (Royal Württemberg) Corps, 4
XXX Corps (United Kingdom), 17

YouTube, 71, 106

www.ingramcontent.com/pod-product-compliance
Lightning Source LLC
Chambersburg PA
CBHW051344040426
42453CB00007B/409